STORES

Retail Display and Design

Retail Store
IMAGE | *Vilma Barr*
Katherine Field

PBC INTERNATIONAL, INC.

Distributor to the book trade in the United States and Canada
Rizzoli International Publications Inc.
through St. Martin's Press
300 Park Avenue South
New York, NY 10010

Distributor to the art trade in the United States and Canada
PBC International, Inc.
One School Street
Glen Cove, NY 11542

Distributor throughout the rest of the world
Hearst Books International
1350 Avenue of the Americas
New York, NY 10019

Library of Congress Cataloging–in–Publication Data

Barr, Vilma
Stores : retail display and design / by Vilma Barr and Katherine Field.
     p.   cm.
  Includes index.
  ISBN 0-86636-339-4 (hardcover : alk. paper) . –– ISBN 0-86636-530-3 (pbk. : alk. paper)
  I. Display of merchandise.   2. Show windows.   3. Stores, Retail––Design and construction.
  I. Field, Katherine, 1960-   II. Title
HF5845.B337   1997   97-20790
659.1'57––dc20   CIP

CAVEAT– Information in this text is believed accurate, and will pose no problem for the student
or casual reader. However, the author was often constrained by information contained in signed
release forms, information that could have been in error or not included at all. Any misinforma-
tion (or lack of information) is the result of failure in these attestations. The author has done
whatever is possible to insure accuracy.

Color separation by AD.VER.srl, Bergamo, Italy
Printing and binding by South China Printing Co. (1988) Ltd., H.K.

10 9 8 7 6 5 4 3 2 1

Printed in Hong Kong

contents

foreword

THIS BOOK REPRESENTS a view of the present as a step into the new millennium. Retail today and in the next few decades will be based on five components: high design, theater, product services, information services (including the Internet) and brand management.

Stores of high design will appeal to the customer who shops with an eye for beauty and style. With their atmosphere of quality, impeccable service, and a specialty in narrow merchandise, these types of stores will always be in demand. They were the shops of royalty 200 years ago, and the shops along the "Avenue" of every major global city—New York, Paris, London, Tokyo, and Rome. These high design stores led the way for the modern retail store.

As stores appeal to new tastes, many are employing theatrical techniques to promote their product. Drama, color, lighting, sound, architecture and display are used to present new store design and merchandise ideas. Such high profile promotional design is visible in the flagship stores of F.A.O. Schwarz, Nike, and Warner Bros., to name a few.

Service remains the key to both today's and tomorrow's success: human interaction—the personal touch—cannot be replaced. From follow-up phone calls, to reaching out into the community, it is imperative that retail not overlook the stroking necessary to retain and build a strong customer base.

Information services includes telecommunications, computerized distribution fulfillment, key to cash registers, warehouse automation, and just-in-time stocking. The Internet is a new horizon in retail; it will enhance and increase retail avenues, broaden worldwide trade and make the global shopping experience a real event. In the near future, we will be able to order canned sturgeon from a Japanese merchant by calling (888) JAPAN FISH or by logging onto the Sturgeon Home Page.

Personal computers and SKU coding have allowed retailers to tightly manage their product lines. Disney, Warner Bros., Nike and Benetton are some of the first to see the way to manage brands and optimize positioning, product and advertisements to drive sales.

Design will always be the genius required to tell the product's story. *Stores: Retail Display and Design* provides a rich palette of ideas which will usher us into the new era.

Dik Glass
Vice President, Store Planning and Construction
F.A.O. Schwarz

introduction

VISUAL MERCHANDISING is both an art and a science, combining elements of subjective creativity and objective merchandising standards.

The merchant/designer team gives the store its visual personality. Together, they create the stage on which the point of presentation leads to the point of purchase, implemented with the most imagination appropriate to the merchandise and the targeted customer base.

Today's intensely competitive retail environment is characterized by sophisticated shoppers who no longer feel a sense of loyalty to established retailers. To succeed in this environment, smart retail managers are utilizing store image as a means of developing customer loyalty and creating long-term profitability. A powerful store image creates a distinctive advantage that is difficult for other retailers to duplicate.

Of course, merchants today are not only competing with each other for the consumer's attention and dollars; they now have to contend with the avalanche of information that hurtles daily through the electronic and print communications channels. Computers, books, magazines, catalogs, radio, and TV relentlessly pump facts and fiction into the information delivery system.

One of the reasons why we have written this book is to provide retailers with a practical tool to better perform in this multichannel milieu—a lively reference of merchandise presentation and store design ideas that can be adapted to keep themselves in their customers' recall mainstreams—like a memorable hangtag between their ears.

THE SELECTION PROCESS

Several hundred excellent projects were submitted by architects, store planners, and interior designers from around the U.S. and from several countries overseas. The exigencies of modern publishing being what they are, we made the final cut to the projects presented in the following pages. We evaluated each store on several criteria:

> *Principles of visual merchandising: balance, repetition, proportion, contrast and dominance • Interior display elements: display cases, platforms, shadowboxes, ledges, islands or environmental settings • Layout • Colors • Lighting • Finishes and materials • Signage • Mannequins and other forms • Size and attractiveness of the entrance*

We next envisioned ourselves as customers responding to the real three-dimensional store. Our checklist included the following questions:

> *Would the design of the space and the displays entice shoppers inside the store or department? • What is the emotional feel of the store: is it fun, entertaining, inspiring? • Does it communicate a congenial atmosphere? • Do the layout and*

the displays make it convenient to locate and examine the merchandise? • Would the store create a lasting impression? Would we as shoppers remember next week what we saw yesterday?

TRENDS

Here are the ten trends that reflect the current thinking on and implementation of projecting a store's image and merchandise positioning:

Keen appreciation of the integration of architectural space with display elements to create a seamless whole. • Fresh graphic interpretations to support the store's logo. • Expanded use of "air rights"—ceiling, tops of walls, corners. • Placement of forms, human or imaginary. • Steel, wood, glass and other materials interpreted in fresh contemporary stylings. • Application of theatrical backgrounds and settings: painting backgrounds dark, walls with murals or print patterns, exposed lighting. • Flexibility, especially for the young market, whose preferences are unpredictable and fast-changing. • Everything can move: showcases, walls, fixtures. • Creative use of interactive electronic technology. • In-store promotions that link merchandise presentations with events. • Combining merchandising with entertainment and dining.

VALUE-ADDED IMAGE

All the image building that a store programs into its operations is intended to provide value-added benefits to shoppers. Give them a place where they are comfortable, where they feel

that the merchant is in tune with their lifestyles, their needs, the way they want to look, furnish their homes, buy the gifts that express their taste and requirements. Reflect the merchandise: the quality, the timeliness, the creativity of the selection.

Give them information and ideas—in books, periodicals, or on a computer screen. Give them access to the Internet, to the World Wide Web. Make their lives fuller, more enjoyable. Keep them up to date, or help them open a new page on history. Give them a place to get away from the frenetic pace of city life, or a place in outlying communities to experience a slice of urban sophistication.

Image is multisensory, multidimensional, and subject to fading without reinforcement. A positive store image is everything the customer perceives. In terms of cause and effect, it will either enhance or severely dent a retailer's bottom line. Turn your image into profit!

Vilma Barr and *Katherine Field*

apparel

DANSKIN FACTORY STORE

GREAT PACIFIC PATAGONIA

BRITCHES GREAT OUTDOORS

FILA FLAGSHIP STORE

LUDWIG BECK

TANGS STUDIO

JESS STORES

BOYD'S

THE LAKE FOREST SHOP BOUTIQUE

THE QUALITY SHOP

BLOOMINGDALE'S

URBAN OUTFITTERS

ANN TAYLOR LOFT

DANSKIN FACTORY STORE

WOODBURY, NEW YORK

A High-energy Outlet

DANSKIN'S OBJECTIVE FOR ITS PROTOTYPE factory store was to appeal to both serious female athletes and women interested in casual exercise. A dance studio theme alludes to Danskin's reputation for dancewear plus its current tagline, "Not just for dancing anymore."

A total store identity was created on a limited budget. Veneer was used in place of wood, and walls were painted. Inexpensive quartz lighting in gymnasium-style lamps hangs from the exposed ceiling.

A quiet, neutral backdrop of wood, creamy paint tones, and natural jute floor covering punches out the bright colors of the small, stretch garments on hangers. Bleacher-style fixtures provide interesting merchandising vignettes and displays. They

Fixture Fabrication

Fleetwood Industries

Construction Manager

S.A. Gavish, Inc.

Contractor

MacDonald Inc.

Lighting Fixtures

Holophane Company

Photo Mural

Chroma Copy

Photographer

©Tom Crane

LEFT *Displays combine dance and exercise props.*

OPPOSITE *A mannequin on a trapeze hovers above the cashwrap desk.*

14

also provide additional storage space which is easily accessible to salespeople. Using the full height of the space, the designers suspended mannequins on overhead horizontal bars and posed them in corners.

A loft-like open ceiling was hung with lamps and punctuated with skylights to take advantage of natural light. Display racks were custom-designed to resemble volleyball net stanchions.

Above the bleachers are blow-ups of athletes and young dancers. In front of the dressing rooms is a 7-foot by 12-foot photomural of a bicyclist overlaid with oak slats to simulate a window. Across the top in brushed steel is the Danskin name and logo.

ABOVE *Danskin's out-let store for exercise and dancewear tingles with energy.*

OPPOSITE *Bleacher-style fixtures give extra dimension to front-facing hanging apparel.*

Fisher Gordon Architects

GREAT PACIFIC PATAGONIA

WASHINGTON, D.C.

The Great Outdoors...Indoors

GREAT PACIFIC PATAGONIA DESIGNS AND PRODUCES technically oriented sports-wear for a variety of outdoor activities, ranging from rock climbing to yacht racing. Its Washington, D.C. store is located in the historic Georgetown section, bordering the Chesapeake and Ohio Canal. An early-nineteenth-century, two-story brick structure plus a 1950s three-story brick-clad addition total 3,800 square feet of selling space.

The company recognized the cultural and esthetic value of the buildings, and was sensitive to their exterior and interior environmental aspects. Exposed brick and wood give warmth and texture throughout the store.

Display Designer
Robert Jarrett

Developer
Germar Properties

Photographer
Alan Karchmer

LEFT *Great Pacific Patagonia's Washington, D.C. store borders the Chesapeake and Ohio Canal in the city's historic Georgetown section.*

OPPOSITE
TOP AND BOTTOM *Two buildings—a two-level structure dating from the early nineteenth century and the other constructed in the 1950s—were combined to create an open and airy 3,800-square-foot store.*

LEFT *Apparel and sports equipment are hung overhead and displayed on wood ledges above the selling floors.*

OPPOSITE *Tables, shelving, and cabinets are made of wood. Stairs between selling floors combine wood and black metal.*

To provide a coherent shopping and merchandising atmosphere, the designers removed the wall between the older building and the newer one and removed all existing interior finishes to allow the building structure to be expressed. The result is an open, airy space with perimeter windows bringing in natural light. Customers have clear horizontal and vertical sight lines to the selling floors. Generous space around the merchandise invites browsing and examination of the items on display.

Tables, shelving, and cabinets are fabricated of wood, as is the cashwrap. The connecting open stairs combine wood and black metal. Recycled pine planks were used for the store's flooring. Dramatic visual effects are achieved by suspending apparel and sports equipment between levels. Wood ledges above the selling floors provide additional display surfaces. Ambient lighting consisting of track lights and exposed compact fluorescent lamps on surface boxes are highly efficient and offer excellent color rendition.

Fisher Gordon Architects

BRITCHES GREAT OUTDOORS

ANNAPOLIS, MARYLAND

Photographer

Alan Karchmer

For Land, For Sea

BRITCHES GREAT OUTDOORS CATERS TO YOUNG, active people who relish the outdoors. Relying on nautical themes, this 1,250-square-foot selling floor gives customers the sensation of entering a sailboat from the starboard side.

Britches' boating theme and its location near the Annapolis waterfront was reinforced by removing the existing second floor, which is now utilized to display merchandise. Small white platforms were installed underneath the windows to enhance the effect. The existing brick floor was exposed and is seen throughout the store, as

LEFT *The bi-level exterior allows shoppers to view merchandise as well as the store's dramatic interior.*

OPPOSITE
TOP LEFT *Merchandise is mounted along the exposed brick walls; floor carts and display tables stagger the store's straight-line layout.*
RIGHT *High ceilings, hanging lights, and wooden beams add to Britches' nautical and sports themes.*

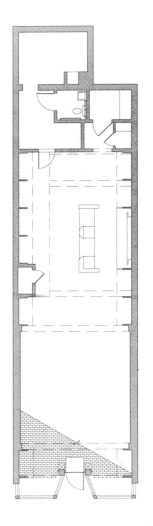

were the original masonry walls. The rough brick juxtaposes with the refined cherry display fixtures. Simulated outdoor lighting helps to enhance Britches' image as a modern active/sportswear retailer.

The narrow hall and high walls are filled with various racks and cubbies to house extra merchandise. Along the center aisle are four lightly stained wooden display tables, a wood-paneled tie rack/cart, and a display rack for featured merchandise.

Imaginari

FILA FLAGSHIP STORE

SAN FRANCISCO, CALIFORNIA

Fila Scores

PROBLEM: THE QUALITY PRODUCTS MADE BY your European-based company, Fila, are widely available, and sold in stores carrying your competitors' products. You want to grow the products' U.S. presence, and develop a retailing identity that will travel to Europe and the Far East. Solution: Tell your designer, "Exercise good taste, and break a few rules."

Fila got what it asked for—a store that seamlessly integrates its line of sport shoes, athletic apparel, and casual sportswear with a design that sets its own course for function and appeal. Located in San Francisco's St. Francis Hotel on Union Square, the Fila Flagship Store scores solidly, adding new techniques to the vocabulary of store design and merchandise presentation. It succeeds handily in achieving its merchandising objectives—to make the products visible and accessible, and to communicate graphically to the customer.

The sculptural central stair was fabricated of stainless steel with Fila logos punched through, giving it lightness and texture. It connects Activewear on the lower level and Sportswear on the upper level. Tensioned stainless steel cables were fashioned into

Correspondent Architect

Freebairn-Smith & Associates

Lighting Consultant

Architectural Lighting Design

General Contractor

Herman/Stewart Construction, Inc.

Photographer

David Patterson

Used by permission only. ©Fila U.S.A., Inc. FILA and the F Design are registered trademarks of Fila Sport S. p. A.

LEFT *Men's shirts are displayed full front on a curved wall. Each aluminum panel is hinged from the top, enabling the stock behind it to be reached.*

OPPOSITE *The sculptural central stair connects Activewear on the lower level and Sportswear on the upper level.*

LEFT *Fila caps on metal pedestals flank the main stairway on both sides.*

the stair's handrails. They are extended to encircle the space around the floor opening of the staircase on the second floor. Back-lit transparencies of Fila posters, logos, and product details lend visual rhythm to the store. Floor fixtures incorporating graphic elements follow the curved walls.

Men's shirts, traditionally stacked by size, are displayed full front on a curved wall. Each aluminum panel that holds the display shirt is hinged from the top and can easily be lifted to reach the stock behind it.

Fila's designer, Kambiz Fard, reconsidered typical shoe displays, and devised a system based on a "shoe ring." The ring attaches to a horizontal panel and holds each shoe on display at an adjustable angle. The resultant effect is of shoes floating in front of the curved walls. Behind each panel is stock of each style.

All shelves have built-in flexibility and can be rearranged by sales associates to adapt to seasonal and holiday merchandise. Feature strip lighting between the wall and the millwork identifies product location and draws the customer's attention.

BELOW *Thousands of Fila logos were punched out of the stainless steel used for the store's core staircase.*

LUDWIG BECK

COLOGNE, GERMANY

Lighting Designer
Ansorg

Contractor
Kaupp + Diether

Photographers
Hans Georg Esch

Palladium Photo Design

A Luminous Display Cube

STRUCTURES WITH BROAD EXPANSES OF GLASS seem to negate the difference between interior and exterior. For those on the outside looking in, observing the activity taking place within the building's transparent enclosure transforms the entire panorama into a giant stage setting. Glass buildings make a singular statement in their surroundings.

They are also hard to ignore, especially when illuminated from within. For the 60,000-square-foot Ludwig Beck store, the image inside is the one that its merchants wanted to project to the outside. Full-height, clear glass windows were installed on the first and second floors, creating a store that is a luminous display cube.

LEFT *In Men's Sportswear, blond wood for the planked floor and fixturing contrasts with the darker hues of the hanging garments.*

OPPOSITE *Full-height, clear glass windows wrap the first and second floors of Ludwig Beck.*

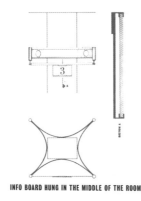

INFO BOARD HUNG IN THE MIDDLE OF THE ROOM

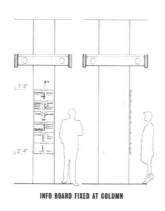

INFO BOARD FIXED AT COLUMN

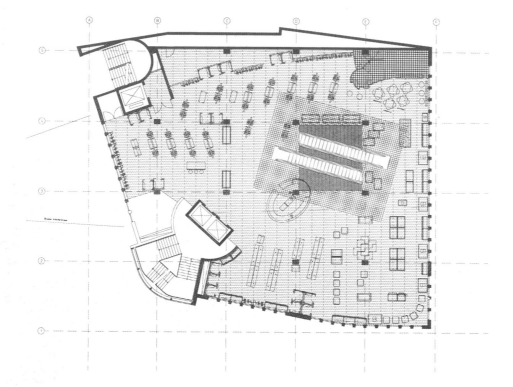

Inside, the store is designed to give shoppers an enjoyable shopping experience. A central oval tower penetrates the selling floors at the same spot on each level. This tower functions as an orientation point for customers and houses the cashwrap station. Store directories and information desks are nearby.

The Men's Sportswear department features blond wood for the planked floor and much of the fixturing. Oversized, angled blond wood frames enclose necktie displays.

As a service to customers, the tower's internal dumbwaiter transports selected merchandise between selling floors and delivers it for final payment on one floor. Customers can shop throughout the store unencumbered by heavy or bulky purchases.

FRCH Design Worldwide

TANGS STUDIO

SINGAPORE

Photographer

Peter Chen

Singapore Chic

TANGS STUDIO OCCUPIES THREE LEVELS totaling 125,000 square feet in Ngee Ann City, an upscale, vertical mall in Singapore's fashionable Orchard Road shopping district. The store carries apparel, footwear, accessories, and items for the home.

Its broad selection is international and eclectic. Bold patterns and tropical colors add to the products' flair and appeal. A background of warm-neutral tones and materials—koto wood, natural shades of marble and terrazzo, and a cream-toned color palette—centers attention on the extensive merchandise mix.

LEFT *A South Seas beach house is replicated for The Island Shop.*

OPPOSITE *Tangs Studio, from the mall's upper level.*

LEFT *A wall-hung cascade of brightly patterned ties draws customers into a men's boutique.*

OPPOSITE *Studio Way collections are positioned along a main aisle. Curved-leg display tables hold accessories.*

The store's open plan offers options for maximum merchandising flexibility and a high degree of visibility on each floor. From the mall's atrium, Tangs Studio is identified with an oversize framed reproduction. Two-story-high decorative lattice work panels flank the central window displays.

The middle and upper levels have a casual ambience. The Island Shop uses Malaysian furniture, teak flooring, an open rafter ceiling, and louvered walls to display women's leisurewear in a beach house environment. At the entrance to a collection of men's casual clothing, a wall display overflows with brightly patterned ties.

Marc-Henri Hecht

JESS STORES

PARIS, FRANCE

Photographer
Studio Clark

French Expression

JESS STORES IS A FRENCH CHAIN OF POPULAR priced men's apparel stores, ranging in size from a 200-square-foot corner boutique to a 2,000-square-foot unit in a shopping center. The architect was commissioned to create a prototype store with fixturing that would fit equally well in all the chain's locations, which also includes sections within department stores.

The store interior had to convey a fresh, straightforward look, reflecting on the merchandise lines carried. To keep within a stringent budget of approximately $10 per square foot, the architect selected basic and simple materials—natural medium-finish wood, white floor tile, and light green linoleum.

The architect introduced white uplight fixtures carrying the store name. Working closely with vendors, he created specially designed fixtures and furniture to accommodate a variety of store configurations and merchandise presentation needs. They were used successfully in Jess windows, and were adaptable to the display of accessories and folded or hanging items.

The Jess image was carried into an area that is usually not treated by store designers. Above the curtained fitting room partitions, the store's logo was interpreted in white neon mounted on a dark plastic base.

LEFT *The store's tight budget was stretched for neon "Jess" signs mounted in the fitting room area.*

OPPOSITE

TOP LEFT AND RIGHT *For the Jess chain of men's sportswear and accessories, the architect created a series of modular fixtures to fit into a variety of store sizes and configurations.* **BOTTOM RIGHT** *A portable metal tube fixture supports a square mirror and white metal grids with peg-hung merchandise.*

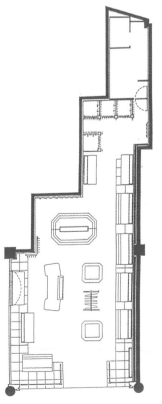

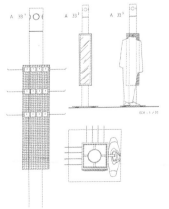

Charles E. Broudy and Associates

BOYD'S

PHILADELPHIA, PENNSYLVANIA

An Impeccable Presentation

BOYD'S, THE LARGEST SPECIALTY MEN'S STORE in Philadelphia, was displaced from its Market Street location when the city claimed the entire block for a downtown improvement program. The owners retained their center city presence by taking over a 60,000-square-foot, c. 1907 building a few blocks away that had been a funeral home.

To succeed in its new location, Boyd's had to appeal to its former clientele plus attract a significant new group of patrons. The store's image as the quality men's

Photographer

Matt Wargo

LEFT *On the outside, blue awnings and canopy establish Boyd's image. The 60,000-square-foot, 90-year-old building was formerly a funeral parlor.*

OPPOSITE *The dark wood of the showcases and shelving units is also used architecturally in this balconied space and throughout Boyd's.*

apparel establishment in the Delaware Valley was the major influence on the design program for the extensive renovation/restoration project.

In addition to completely rehabilitating all of the building's systems—electric, HVAC, plumbing, vertical transportation, life safety code, and structural engineering—selling floors and tailoring workrooms had to be created from the former undertaking establishment.

Boyd's image starts at the curb. A blue canopy with the store name in gold is an impressive introduction. Four show windows facing the street were added. Each of the store's windows on all four levels was fitted with a blue awning, a decorative addition to the Beaux-Arts facade.

The architect conserved existing materials and details. A dramatic bi-level space was created by opening up the first floor ceiling and connecting the two floors with a contemporary stairway. Fixtures and showcases are of dark wood. In addition, Boyd's installed a cafe for its customers, following the trend of cafes-within-stores.

BELOW *Following its extensive renovation and restoration, Boyd's gained a new, elegant image as the Delaware Valley's quality men's apparel store.*

OPPOSITE *The dramatic first floor and mezzanine has a semi-circular reception/greeters station facing the entry.*

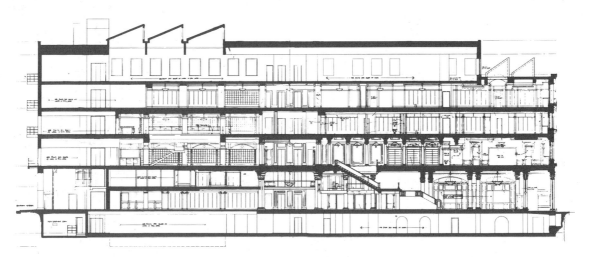

Contractor
Altounian Builders, Inc.

Photographer
Michael Roberts

THE LAKE FOREST SHOP BOUTIQUE

LAKE FOREST, ILLINOIS

Etched in Elegance

THE LAKE FOREST SHOP IS A 70-YEAR-OLD, family-owned women's fashion boutique that has been a long-standing tradition in Lake Forest, an upscale Chicago suburb. Catering to a loyal following, it sells business apparel, gowns, and designer dresses with its own private label. A new merchandise category, "Generation 5," appeals to younger customers.

When the store underwent remodeling, the owners wanted to enhance the sophisticated quality of the merchandise without making major architectural changes. The designers' solution was an elegant ambiance achieved with contemporary lighting and a palette of fine finishes and materials, including new carpeting, damask wall covering, jacquard upholstery fabrics, marble, wood flooring, and etched glass.

The color scheme, which was changed from earth tones to off-white, light gray, pink, and mauve, was applied to the carpet, marble display window platforms, laminated riser cubes, fabric-wrapped panels, and fitting room drapery. Softening the

LEFT *The elegant ambiance of the remodeled Lake Forest Shop was achieved with new lighting and a palette of fine finishes and materials.*

OPPOSITE

TOP *Narrow vertical glass panels with an alternating pattern of etched and clear horizontal stripes provide the owner with a view of the sales floor from her office.*

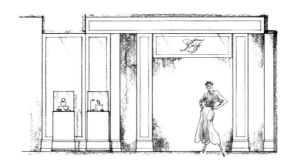

merchandise background was cost-effectively achieved by installing fabric-wrapped panels between repainted existing surface-mounted chrome standards.

Clear etched glass sign panels were designed to "float," creating a delicate shadow against the soft off-white walls. The Lake Forest Shop's logo was etched in glass and installed as header dividing the front of the shop from the rear. Narrow vertical glass panels with an alternating pattern of etched and clear horizontal stripes provide the owner with a view of the sales floor from her office. Delicately etched outlines of iris flowers at the top of transparent divider panels draw attention to a merchandise display.

Large existing track light fixtures were replaced with MR-16 lamps that improve the quality of the light within the space and add depth and dimension to the merchandise.

Contractor

**Marquis
Construction**

Photographer

Glen McClure

Fleeger Inc.

THE QUALITY SHOP

VIRGINIA BEACH, VIRGINIA

Relaxed Elegance

NEAR THE TOP OF THE LIST OF CHALLENGES facing specialty retailers today is how to maintain a high-quality image without sacrificing flexibility. With "quality" the operative word in its name, the owners of this retail store had a heritage of excellence to maintain. For the third Quality Shop, the designers created a setting that is an extension of the casually elegant merchandise selection, and also reflects the emphasis on service.

Merchandise typically available only in larger metropolitan areas is a specialty, such as European lines and a broad selection of sizes, including large sizes, and sportswear. An expanded sportswear grouping is an important category.

Two interior "buildings," one an enclosure for clothing and the other for the tailor shop, were constructed within the space. An undulating wall of copper sheeting encloses the clothing section. For the tailor shop, however, the owners wanted to give customers a view into this traditional backroom operation. Here, the care that is taken

LEFT *The fixturing program affords flexibility for merchandise presentation such as positioning of swimwear during warm weather and formal wear for the holidays.*

OPPOSITE *An interior perspective is created by diamond-pattern floor inserts of the store's logo, decreasing in size to the steps at the rear.*

to custom-fit each customer's purchase to his satisfaction is visible through large windows.

Z-shaped slotwall units are not on walls but on wheels, and feature slots spaced six inches on center. Copper-plated hardware on the units complements the store's copper walls and copper interior and exterior accents. A maple grid extends above display cubes for ties and shirts.

Lighting creates a visual ceiling. Ambient light is supplemented by fixtures with color-corrected fluorescent lamps mounted on black grids. Ceiling fans supply energy-efficient cooling and add to the mixture of traditional and contemporary design elements.

BELOW *Antiques, used as working fixtures, are combined with customized "Shaker-modern" pieces.*

OPPOSITE
TOP *Cashwrap area features are used to present accessories.*
BOTTOM LEFT *Maple tables are coordinated with wood-finished slotwall.*
BOTTOM RIGHT *Stained glass panels are installed above the louvred doors.*

BLOOMINGDALE'S

BLOOMINGTON, MINNESOTA

The Natural Choice

BLOOMINGDALE'S AT THE MALL OF AMERICA achieves a special design distinction with its adaptation of the region's turn-of-the-century Prairie School of architecture, incorporating detailing and forms seen in buildings such as those designed by Frank Lloyd Wright. The interior of the 210,000-square-foot store is characterized by strong geometric forms and liberal use of natural materials. From the atrium's upper level, strategically devised sight lines draw shoppers' attention to surrounding merchandise displays.

On the first floor, Men's Clothing provides a warm club atmosphere, with dark brown parquet wood floors and a plush center-stage couch. An oriental carpet defines

Architects

Diedrich Architects and Associates

Lighting Designer

David Apfel

Photographer

Don DuBroff

LEFT *Bloomingdale's upper level entrance at The Mall of America.*

OPPOSITE

TOP *The Men's Suits department has traditional club-like elegance.*
BOTTOM LEFT *A wooden arch embedded with a mirrored panel houses a display on both shelves and a coat rack behind wooden display tables.*
BOTTOM RIGHT *The Gold Card Room adds elegance and comfort for Bloomingdale's special customers.*

the seating area and a steel-framed display table. Wall panels behind the seating area and merchandise racks are covered with gray linen, which creates a textural transition between the flat surfaces of the walls and the merchandise itself. A wooden arch frames a mirrored panel with shelving.

Women's Suits offers a strong contemporary contrast. Here, a neon-accented dropped ceiling and patterned floor design visually define the merchandise displays and the grouped mannequins.

On the third floor a lounge area is set aside for the special Bloomingdale's customer. The Gold Card Room was inspired by the 1930s classic interior design of New York's Radio City Music Hall, with lightly stained wood panels, tan seating, and a black marble kitchenette.

Pompei A.D.

URBAN OUTFITTERS

CHICAGO, ILLINOIS

Contractor

Plant Construction

Special Finishes and Materials

Otto Installations

Photographer

Micheal P. McLaughlin

An Urban Approach

URBAN OUTFITTERS HAS BECOME A MERCHANDISING powerhouse by catering to its target market of 18-to-30-year-olds. Each Urban Outfitters store is site-specific, adapting to the distinct characteristics of the existing building and the surrounding community. As *The New York Times* observed, "...Urban Outfitters has managed to co-opt antiestablishment consumers in their teens and 20's by giving them a shopping experience that embraces them."

Merchandise assortment in Urban Outfitters' 11,500-square-foot store in Chicago's "Gold Coast" shopping area ranges from casual apparel to area rugs, lamps, and handmade stationery. The lofty two-floor store was designed as part warehouse, part garage,

LEFT AND OPPOSITE TOP *The exterior of Urban Outfitters, Chicago, relates to the surrounding city environment.*

OPPOSITE

BOTTOM *Blue jeans "stand" in mid-air, supported by a flat plastic cover and wood backing.*

part feed store. Architectural features were integrated with merchandise presentation wherever possible. Shelves of blue jeans are stacked against a yellow-washed wall, forming a horizontal grid beneath vertical steel channels. The channels are decorated with framed compositions: for example, a pair of jeans is positioned like ready-made art on corrugated metal. Below, a shoe display radiates from painted steel barrels.

Above the selling floor, the 24-foot-high ceiling is punctuated with skylights. The designers exposed overhead girders, juxtaposing industrial materials such as steel with the earthiness of raw, distressed wood. Vertical circulation was achieved by carving a massive opening into the second floor deck and hanging a steel platform that functions as a display/sales area.

In-store graphics campaigns are changed frequently to maintain an atmosphere of constant evolution. The Chicago store was designed to allow maximum space for these displays with areas for hanging posters and walls of plate glass onto which graphics are silkscreened directly, visible from the outside. One recent campaign turned playbills advertising local clubs and bands into collages and case displays. Store associates are encouraged to be creative with displays. They exercise their own judgment in positioning signs and posters to best suit their store's promotional approach.

LEFT *Exposed architectural elements enhance the casual look that appeals to the store's under-30 target market.*

OPPOSITE

TOP LEFT *The massed T-shirt display reinforces the product shown on the foreground mannequins.*

TOP RIGHT *Mannequins are positioned on the raised metal platform beneath a colorful sign.*

BOTTOM *Displays visually divide the store's 24-foot-high space and allow customers to orient themselves and locate merchandise.*

ANN TAYLOR LOFT

RIVERHEAD, NEW YORK

Lofty Aspirations

THE TYPICAL OFF-PRICE OUTLET'S REPUTATION of plain pipe racks and exposed fluorescent fixtures is becoming history. Image-conscious Ann Taylor developed a separate division with its own brand identity and distinct line of off-price merchandise. Lower price points appeal to a targeted market that is younger than the typical Ann Taylor customer.

To communicate this format in the 12,500-square-foot Ann Taylor Loft, the aura of an informal but sophisticated urban loft was created: white-washed brick walls, exposed trusses, industrial-type ceiling fixtures, and concrete flooring. Natural light is introduced by a wall of windows along the store's front and from overhead skylights. The color and materials palette is composed of navy blue, tan, brushed nickel, and

Contractor

Park/Retail Design

Photographer

Andrew Bordwin

LEFT *The tan brick exterior with blue panel trim coordinates with the color palette of the selling floor.*

OPPOSITE *The 12,500-square-foot Ann Taylor Loft outlet store features skylights, exposed trusses, concrete floor, and movable display fixtures.*

natural wood, with maple-trimmed display fixtures.

A flexible fixturing system can be reconfigured to meet seasonal and special merchandise presentation needs. The horizontal store envelope is divided into three areas, with petites and shoes on either side of the main selling floor. Along the perimeter are flexible wood and nickel display units on which are hung mirrors and ladders on tracks; merchandise is displayed on both sides to facilitate self-service. Facing the front entrance is a wood-frame table divided into seven segments on top with a double tier of white wire-front baskets beneath containing additional stock.

accessories

GIORGIO BEVERLY HILLS

CARLOS FALCHI

LA MAISON SIMONS

HUSH PUPPIES DIRECT

NEX.IS

MARK CROSS OUTLET STORE

BLOOR STREET HOSIERY

ALAIN MIKLI/OPTIQUE

Jon Greenberg & Associates Inc.

GIORGIO BEVERLY HILLS

BEVERLY HILLS, CALIFORNIA

A Sunny Showcase

THE EXPANSION AND REMODELING of Giorgio Beverly Hills on Rodeo Drive created a natural light-filled 6,200-square-foot store, more than twice as large as the original boutique. Apparel, accessories, and gifts are displayed in a gallery-like setting that combines the influences of both California and Tuscany.

The pale aqua ceiling, Mankata stone floors, and color-pigmented, smooth plaster walls in sunny yellows and creams all assist the illusion of bringing the outside

Millwork and Fixtures

Lahser Contract Matrix Store Fixtures, Inc.

Lighting Consultant

Gary Steffy Lighting Design

General Contractor

Altered Spaces, Inc.

Photographer

Stephen Graham

LEFT
The exterior facade has a deeply carved frame around the windows and entrance.

OPPOSITE *A skylight introduces natural light to the Italian street-like setting in the bath products area.*

indoors. An interior courtyard has a skylight arcade, flagstone-finished floors, and a trickling fountain that lead to the Giorgio boutique at the back of the store. The atrium walls are stucco.

Geometric cutouts were carved out of the store's walls, giving the selling floor almost a street facade appeal. They also visually expand the store and give customers glimpses between rooms. Ambient illumination from overhead fixtures is augmented by showcase and feature lighting above and behind the wall cutouts.

ABOVE *A gallery-like setting for apparel, accessories, and gifts is influenced by both California and Tuscany.*

CARLOS FALCHI

DALLAS, TEXAS

Visuals
Alden D. Clanahan

Graphic Designers
LGF Design Studio

Lighting Designer
World's Away

Developer
NorthPark Center

Contractor
RCR Construction

Fixture Production
JT&L Co.

Aquarium
Aquatic Designs

Photographer
Steve Foxall

Bold, Magical, and Fun

EVERY INCH OF HIS 1,100-SQUARE-FOOT BOUTIQUE carries the personal imprint of Brazilian-born designer Carlos Falchi. Vibrant colors and surprises are everywhere. Showcased in the store are women's accessories—couture, mid-price, and Falchi's signature collection.

Falchi compares his store to a painting, in that he combines different shapes and sources of light to make an impact. The basic palette of red, blues, green, and black is accented with pink, orange, and mauve. Multicolored hand-broken pieces of acrylic create a vibrant floor mosaic in the entryway, a pattern that is repeated in the custom carpet. Raw silk covers the wall and bay paneling.

LEFT *The entry to Carlos Falchi's boutique is marked by a glass-enclosed light-box display.*

OPPOSITE *The 1,100-square-foot store is a panoply of colors and patterns into which the merchandise is integrated.*

The 13-foot-high vaulted ceiling, which was painted by Mr. Falchi, features suspended starburst-perforated teak lighting fixtures. An aquarium—flanked on either side by shelving—is filled with vividly colored saltwater fish, and sits on top of built-in storage cabinets painted in six bright colors and accented with copper swirls.

LEFT *Copper swirls decorate the jewelry display unit beneath cubbies holding purses and handbags.*

OPPOSITE

TOP *Exotic patterns and brilliant hues frame and support a saltwater fish tank flanked by display shelves.*
BOTTOM LEFT *The 13-foot-high vaulted ceiling painted by Mr. Falchi is punctuated by starburst teak fixtures and downlights.*
BOTTOM RIGHT *The entry's mosaic pattern and colors are interpreted as part of the red carpet, drawing customers to the store's inner recesses.*

Architect

Michael Alain

Contractor

TMC Construction

Photographer

Design Archive/Robert Burley

LA MAISON SIMONS

QUEBEC CITY, CANADA

High-fashion's Classic Approach

FOR A RECENT COMPLETE RENOVATION AND EXPANSION (from 25,000 square feet to over 45,000 square feet), La Maison Simons, a premier contemporary apparel retailer, chose a classic design and display theme. The designers' challenge was to facilitate traffic flow from several mall entrances as well as an exterior entrance, while creating a distinctive and unmistakable fashion presence within the mall itself.

The final result of their efforts accomplishes those goals and much more. The central focus of the store is the rotunda, which is defined by Ionic columns and arches. It features a 38-foot-high classical dome structure. The dome's ceiling is enhanced by a custom-commissioned fresco that is framed by downlighting and punctured with

LEFT *White Ionic columns mark the exterior and mall entrances to La Maison Simons.*

OPPOSITE *Defined by Ionic columns and arches, the rotunda's fresco is framed with downlighting and punctured with circular windows.*

circular windows. It has become a must-see destination for mall shoppers.

Controlled application of detailed architecture is utilized to emphasize displays within each department. Unique architectural elements are also used strategically at intersections of aisles, along walls, and within departments to create focus. The generous ceiling height and the monumental nature of the space, combined with luxurious materials and attention to detail, create an impressive backdrop that accentuates quality fashion merchandising.

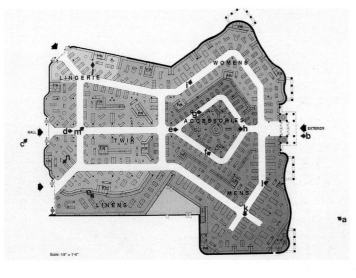

Scale: 1/8" = 1'-0"

Contractor

**Jaycon
Development
Corporation**

Photographer

**Mark Steele,
Fitch Inc.**

Fitch Inc.

HUSH PUPPIES DIRECT

VERO BEACH, FLORIDA

New Directions for a Classic

HUSH PUPPIES APPEALED TO THE "green generation" even before the environmental movement became widespread. Wolverine World Wide, Hush Puppies' parent company, recognized that their shoes were the comfort shoe of choice for a loyal following. To capture a broader market, they decided to invest in a new retail image. Hush Puppies Direct is the company's strategy to extend the brand identity to a younger and more fashion-conscious shopper.

All forms of graphic communications were recreated to reflect a contemporary image in the 3,000-square-foot store. The basset hound likeness that has long been a brand identity was retained because of its familiarity to retailers and consumers. In addition to fresh packaging, labeling, and merchandising materials, the strategy includes a new children's line and a new design approach for company-owned retail stores.

LEFT *Hush Puppies Direct supports the brand's new design approach with natural materials and lifestyle photography.*

OPPOSITE

TOP *The selling floor and the dropped ceiling of connected wood panels are both made of light-finish wood.*
BOTTOM *An updated graphic image targets a younger, more fashion-conscious shopper.*

LEFT *The cashwrap in the 3,000-square-foot, company-owned Hush Puppies Direct store.*

OPPOSITE *The Pups line has its own corner sales area; the circular try-on unit is on casters.*

Hush Puppies Direct tells its current story with natural materials, lifestyle photography enlargements, and two- and three-dimensional reproductions of the basset hound. Light-finish wood is used throughout the store—for the floor, cashwrap, display tables, seating, and the frames around wall shelf units. A dropped ceiling of wood panels features solid panels alternating with panels containing downlighting.

The store is segmented into four areas, from front to back: casual; career casual; outside; and comfort dress. In the center, four floor fixtures highlight one of each of the product lines and display seasonal merchandise and special promotions. Pups, the children's line, has its own corner sales area which is defined by a semi-circular overhead canopy.

HUSH PUPPIES® **PuPS**

WE'VE
GOT
your
SIZE
AND
WIDTH

If we don't have your size in
stock but we make them,
we'll special order and send
them to you in no time.

NEX.IS

SINGAPORE

Quick-change Flexibility

WHAT DO 15-TO 25-YEAR-OLDS IN SINGAPORE really want? Something hip and cutting edge, or something anti-fashion? Will today's trend be tomorrow's markdown? A retailer catering to this churning customer base definitely has to be a quick-change artist as well as a savvy merchandiser.

Nex.is, a major player in this market, is a 20,000-square-foot store with built-in flexibility to follow its customers' taste preferences. The designers developed a number of

LEFT *Nex.is was designed to keep pace with the trends and impulse buying that characterize its young target market customers.*

OPPOSITE

TOP *Free-standing wood and metal display tables and wood shelf units can be easily reconfigured.* **BOTTOM** *Surrounding a structural column is a CD music station, part of the Nex.is shopping experience.*

80

generic fixtures that could be adapted to the open-plan layout. Since there are no walls, shoppers look overhead for round signs hung from the ceiling to identify the departments.

Dressing rooms are modular; they can be moved, ganged, or temporarily stored. Instead of traditional floor-mounted showcases, Nex.is has free-standing wood and metal display tables that can be easily reconfigured. Drawer pulls in whimsical shapes are a delightful detail.

BELOW LEFT AND RIGHT *Generic fixtures throughout Nex.is can be adapted to the store's open-plan layout. Dressing rooms are portable.*

Nex.is, located in Singapore's Scotts Shopping Centre, is a 20,000-square-foot destination store for apparel and accessories appealing to the city's 15-to-25-year-old population.

Photographer

Andrew Bordwin

Desgrippes Gobé & Associates

MARK CROSS OUTLET STORE

WEST READING, PENNSYLVANIA

A New Game

MARK CROSS, THE OLDEST LEATHER GOODS manufacturer in the U.S. (its founding date of 1845 is part of the logo), also operates retail shops. Customers have grown to expect that the products bearing the company's name and the store in which they are purchased carry a special message of quality and reliability. The designers of the firm's outlet store in eastern Pennsylvania were well aware of the Mark Cross tradition, and its elite niche in the country's business history. This store, located in a popular outlet shopping district, would be equally appropriate for an upscale big-city shopping neighborhood.

Its symmetrical layout is based on horseshoe configurations of the women's department on one side and men's on the other, facing into the central gifts area. The merchandise assortment includes gloves, umbrellas, ties, women's handbags, attaché

LEFT *White walls, dark wood fixtures, a brown and white checkerboard floor, and pedestals resembling oversized chess pieces are the main design themes.*

OPPOSITE

TOP *The store's symmetrical plan has a central gifts area with the women's department on one side and the men's on the other, both with horseshoe configurations.*
BOTTOM *Detail of clear dome top display on an oversized chess piece pedestal.*

cases, desk accessories, and gifts.

Against a background of white walls and dark wood fixtures is a bold, brown and white checkerboard floor. Pedestals shaped like oversized brown and white chess pieces display gift items viewed under clear domes.

The light/dark grid pattern becomes three-dimensional for a wall of dark wood shadow box displays of women's handbags and gifts. Customers can also examine handbags in display showcases with hinged lift-up tops. Drawer units beneath hold back-up stock. Luggage items are displayed on a triple-tiered rolling cart detailed with gold-tone metal mesh on two sides.

II By IV Design Associates

Contractor
Riteway
Contracting

Photographer
David Whittaker

BLOOR STREET HOSIERY

TORONTO, CANADA

An Underground Showcase

BECAUSE THIS 650-SQUARE-FOOT STORE IS LOCATED in an underground shopping center beneath one of Toronto's windiest corners, its ceiling mural reveals people who seem to be walking across the ceiling. The mural is set into a shallow mirrored bulkhead that suggests a skylight.

Bloor Street Hosiery is a privately owned, multi-line hosiery operation carrying hosiery ranging in price from $2 to $175 per pair, plus representative apparel items. The assignment given to the designers was to set the store apart from the proliferation of hosiery franchise operations, without exceeding $65 per square foot, all inclusive. They succeeded with flying colors: a four-fold increase in sales was recorded from the

LEFT *Shoppers see inside the underground store through the front windows that are curved at the top and angled on the sides.*

OPPOSITE
TOP *The keystone-shaped ceiling mural simulates foot traffic above the store.*
BOTTOM *Elliptical signs identifying product lines are held in place by taut black cord frames with center tassels.*

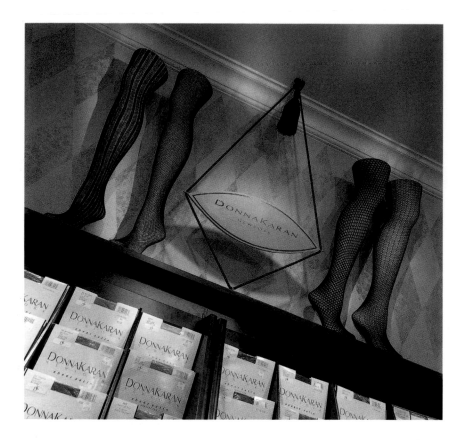

LEFT *The geometric identifying signs draw attention to the merchandise displays.*

OPPOSITE
TOP *Existing stepped-back hosiery racks were reconfigured with wide angles to soften their silhouette and create interest in the store's straight-line plan.*
BOTTOM *Upward-flaring maple display fixtures are brightened with a stenciled gold design.*

shop's previous facility during a comparable period. In addition, the shopping center's management uses Bloor Street Hosiery as a showcase for prospective tenants.

Clear site lines to the main product display inside are seen through the front windows that are curved at the top and angled at the sides. Above the entry is an elliptical gold-backed sign with the store name in a stylized contemporary typeface.

Budget constraints required reusing the existing stepped-back black hosiery racks. To soften their silhouette, the designers used wide angles to create interest in the straight-line plan. Signs identifying product lines are elliptical, set into tasseled cord frames.

Floor fixtures and the cashwrap flare upward gently from plinth bases. Gold stencils applied to the maple cabinetry add a dash of elegant sparkle. Display pedestals are set on round swirled black metal feet. On the walls, a hand-painted harlequin pattern executed in soft peach and tan adds to the fresh and sophisticated environment.

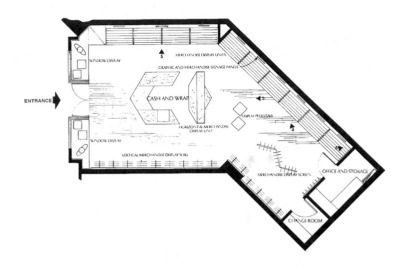

Tobin/Parnes Design Enterprises

ALAIN MIKLI/OPTIQUE

NEW YORK CITY

A Gallery for Designer Eyewear

THE 50 BLOCKS OF NEW YORK CITY'S Madison Avenue from 45th Street to 95th Street are famous for upscale shopping. With world-class boutiques lining both sides of the Avenue—interrupted by assorted restaurants, pharmacies, and other services patronized by area residents—competition to gain shoppers' attention is spirited.

Alain Mikli, with retail stores in Paris and Tokyo, understands projecting a visual image that is unexpected and exceptional is important in building and maintaining market share. For its upper Madison Avenue location, two small adjoining spaces were joined to form a three-dimensional canvas of shapes and arrangements that give the eyewear on display a value-added gallery-setting.

The designers created a sharply tapered triangular configuration and built the store's internal rhythm around it. Bearing a resemblance to Foucault's pendulum, their creation is fashioned in blond wood with a darker tip. In full-circle configuration, it is suspended from black top consultation tables, and supported by black metal

90

Contractor
Richter & Ratner

Photographer
Chun Y Lai

LEFT *Tall glass windows provide a showcase for the store inside.*

OPPOSITE *A pointed dark-tipped sculptural form contributes to the look at Alain Mikli's upper Madison Avenue store in New York.*

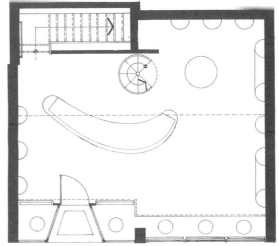

LEFT *The store's signature pendulum-like shape serves as a wall-mounted base beneath curved-glass display cases and mirrors.*

OPPOSITE *A black metal spiral staircase leads to the office and work area on the balcony. Its shape repeats the curved counter and customer chairs and stools.*

frames for sculptural window display stands. The half-circle variation is wall-mounted beneath curved- glass display cases and mirrors that are framed in the same blond wood.

The curved shape is repeated for the counter and customer chairs and stools. Above the selling floor is a balcony office and work area, which can be reached by a black metal spiral staircase. The walls are painted a pale yellow that adds additional warmth to the wood furniture, display cases, and movable storage units, as well as to the natural-finish wood floor.

kids

TWINKLES

MCLEAN, VIRGINIA

Contractor
Monarc Construction

Photographer
Alan Karchmer

A Castle on a Budget

TWINKLES' SPECIALIZED MARKET NICHE is imported children's clothing. The owners wanted a distinctive ambience on a very tight budget of $75,000 for the 1,100-square-foot store. As a small tenant in the sprawling Tysons Corner Shopping Center in suburban Washington, D.C., the store design for Twinkles would have to be memorable on its own and help to establish an image for the merchandise.

A mythical medieval castle was adapted as the theme for the store interior and the display elements. Accessories and the cashwrap station are incorporated into the castle-top cabinetry at the store's center. Taking their cue from the store name, Twinkles'

LEFT *Twinkles is interpreted in pink neon script to create a standout storefront.*

OPPOSITE
RIGHT AND FAR RIGHT *Spotlights and uplighting emphasize the vaulted ceiling and add to Twinkles' contemporary fairy-tale ambience.*
BOTTOM LEFT *Display towers with stylized castle-like tops surround the white cashwrap.*

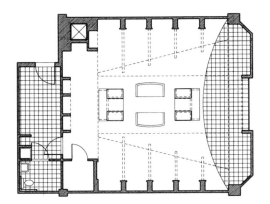

designers created sandblasted stars at the storefront, sprinkled gold stars against the blue ceiling, and installed quartz lighting at the vault over the center cashwrap.

Lighting fixtures fill an important role at Twinkles. Uplights with fluted white metal shades bounce light off the blue and white ceiling, providing uniform illumination that is flattering to both the merchandise and shoppers. Spotlights suspended on delicate pendants focus interest on displayed items, and contribute to the store's contemporary fairy-tale look.

OILILY

TROY, MICHIGAN

Contractor

**Bren Mar
Construction**

Photographer

Balthazar Korab

A Sophisticated Country Environment

OILILY SPECIALIZES IN COLORFUL, ETHNIC-PATTERNED CLOTHING for women
and children made in The Netherlands. The store also carries a full line of fashion
accessories and body care products. The clothing fuses the sunny qualities of folk
art with high fashion, while the light-finished wood display elements and balanced
placement of provincial graphic icons create a sophisticated country look.

From the mall entrance, customers have a clear view of the store through full-
height mullionless windows. The three-dimensional store name on the windows is
mounted between bands of pattern.

The designers created fanciful, bright symbols to integrate the patterns and colors
of the clothing with the store design. The images appear on the maple walls at the

LEFT *The Oilily mall
entrance utilizes tall
glass windows to estab-
lish its image and give
shoppers a clear view
of merchandise inside
the well-lit store.*

OPPOSITE *Exposed
and hidden soffits as
well as ceiling-mounted
fixtures spread light
over merchandise while
bringing out textures
and colors.*

LEFT *A mannequin within a curtained frame brightens a corner at Oilily.*

OPPOSITE *Patterned header caps frame a shoe display shelf. A child-sized pedestal is in the foreground.*

entrance and are featured on the fixtures throughout the store, including headers over the shoe and apparel display shelf units.

Children's clothing is also displayed in freestanding enclosed garment racks which are designed to resemble steamer trunks, a delightful touch that adds to the international flair of the Oilily collection. The wall fixtures have shelves and backs of clear-finish northern maple. They frame the merchandise and contribute dimension and importance to the items on display.

Skillfully organized lighting creates an overall warmth in the store environment, achieved through hidden cove-lighting, exposed bulbs mounted into soffits, and pendant-suspended wall-washers.

Fitzpatrick Design Group, Inc.

DAYTON HUDSON

BURNSVILLE, MINNESOTA

Lighting Designer

**Merchandise
Lighting Inc.**

Architect

**Bentz, Thompson,
Rietow, Inc.**

Photographer

Don DuBroff

Kids in Color!

DO CHILDREN DREAM IN COLOR? If they do, they can relate to the Kids department in Dayton Hudson's Burnsville Shopping Center store. The second floor department was part of the 50,000-square-foot store's remodeling program.

Kids is bright, glossy and fun. Against a predominantly white background, liberal use of red and yellow creates a strong presentation theme. Overhead neon directs customers down the tri-color pathway to draped red and yellow tabletop displays.

Illuminated signs side-mounted on red-striped center columns graphically identify the size ranges. High-gloss red panels provide the backdrop for the wall-mounted hanger bars facing the aisle and frame the backlit rear display area.

LEFT *The exterior
of the remodeled
Dayton Hudson store
in the Burnsville
Shopping Center,
Burnsville, Minnesota.*

OPPOSITE

TOP *The bright red
mannequins on a
glossy red circular base
are reflected against a
mirrored backdrop.*
BOTTOM *Red, white,
and yellow tones
occur throughout the
Kids department.*

Contractor

**Dickenson
Cameron
Construction**

Photographer

Paul Bielenberg

FRCH Design Worldwide

LONDON FOG KIDS

GILROY, CALIFORNIA

From a Child's Perspective

WITH ITS CHEERFUL COLORS, PLAYFUL SHAPES, skewed proportions, and unexpected angles, the London Fog Kids factory outlet store is retailing from a child's perspective. Located in the Outlets at Gilroy, 40 miles south of Palo Alto, the 2,300-square-foot store appeals to both adults and their children.

Boys clothing is displayed on the left; girls is on the right. Sizes progress from infants to toddlers at the front of the store up to size 14 at the rear.

The color palette features robin's egg blue and lemon-yellow walls; fixtures are stained in shades of peach, red, blue, and green; and the flooring is blue-speckled rubber. Basic geometric shapes that give the store the feeling of a large playroom were utilized for the fixtures, cashwrap, and feature walls. At the front of the store is a free-standing fixture that resembles a sawhorse. The lime-green cashwrap in the middle of the store is a fanciful boat/car hybrid. Soft-form mannequins shown on wood platforms are mounted on casters for easy maneuverability.

LEFT *Shoppers can preview the 2,300-square-foot London Fog Kids store beyond its clear glass facade.*

OPPOSITE
TOP *The focal wall display has dual-level eye-appeal to attract adult shoppers and their children.*
BOTTOM LEFT *A multi-level display fixture is mounted on toy wagon wheels.*
BOTTOM RIGHT *A rope-and-pulley stretched horizontally within a natural-finished wood frame displays merchandise attached with clothespins.*

A perimeter fixture system takes its cue from construction equipment. The focal wall in the girls and infants section displays merchandise on a block-like form suspended on pulleys that looks like a large, interactive toy. In the boys section, wedge-shape wood fixtures are suspended by ropes on pulleys, mounted against eight-inch-thick backdrops. The rope-and-pulley system, stretched horizontally between a natural wood frame, displays hanging merchandise attached with clothespins.

Around the store's perimeter is a maple Shaker-style wall rail. Wood pegs hold clothing and accessories, while the rail itself divides the walls into selling and non-selling areas. In the rear of the store, there is a children's play area with a chalkboard, picnic table and benches so that youngsters can amuse themselves while their parents are completing the transactions at the cashwrap.

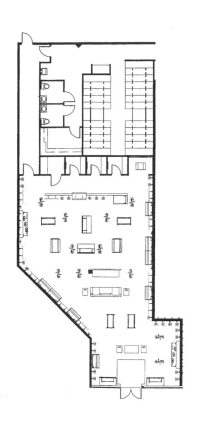

THE TORTOISE AND THE HARE

NEW YORK CITY

Lighting Designer

Lighting Collaborative Inc.

Contractor

S. Macedo Construction Corporation

Display Fabrication

Hudson Scenic Studio, Inc.

Photographer

Timothy Higgins

Interactive...Whimsical...and Fun!

THE TORTOISE AND THE HARE, A 640-SQUARE-FOOT children's hair cutting salon that also sells gifts, toys, and hair care products, communicates visually with youngsters in their own language. Oversized, eye-catching graphics, exuberant colors, kid-scaled furniture, and computer games keep the shop's young customers entertained.

The entrance is defined by a handpainted portal "hedge," from which emerge the legendary tortoise and hare. Each mirrored barber station—there are two double stations for older children and a single infants' station—is like a stage set. Oversize Lego blocks surrounded one double station; the other is defined by eight-foot-tall crayons at the sides and crisscrossed rulers at the top. Three-and-a-half-foot-long combs and scissors hang from the ceiling. Cabinets containing interactive game equipment are built into each station, fitted with remote controls that extend to the chairs.

A four-foot-high working clock in the shape of a pocket watch is centered on the back wall. Vinyl floor tiles of solid red, yellow, and blue coordinate with off-white tiles splattered with primary colors.

LEFT *A painted hedge containing the hare on one side and the tortoise on the opposite side frame the entrance.*

OPPOSITE
TOP LEFT AND RIGHT *The shop's lively interior features an interplay of bright colors and geometric shapes, oversized combs and scissors suspended from the ceiling, and a four-foot-high working pocket watch on the wall.*
CENTER *The reception desk is between two merchandise displays.*
BOTTOM RIGHT *Each station contains built-in interactive game equipment regulated by the young customers operating remote controls.*

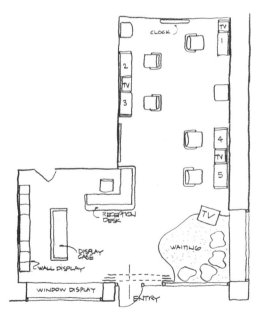

THE GREAT TRAIN STORE

ALBANY, NEW YORK

Selling Railroad Nostalgia

THE GREAT TRAIN STORE CELEBRATES THE ENDURING lure of railroading with its selection of model trains, gifts, toys, hobby materials, apparel, books, videotapes, and memorabilia. Elaborate train layouts, moving electric trains on overhead trestles, train whistles and sounds, and audiovisual presentations give the space an exciting and interactive atmosphere that encourages shoppers to enter and browse. Moreover, the 2,000-square-foot store is specifically merchandised to be compatible with local railroad history and market characteristics.

The storefront is constructed of wood and glass with a design which integrates the internal decor and color palette. Dark wood shelving and display units and wood plank flooring are reminiscent of vintage waiting rooms in small-town railway stations. Large-scale moving trains on an overhead trestle encircle the interior and, in many stores, the exterior facade.

Display Designer
Schuette Cabinet, Inc.

Models and Layouts
Missouri Rail Systems

Electrical and Mechanical Engineers
Q & W Associates

Contractor
Storecrafters, Inc.

Developer
Pyramid Companies

Photographer
Elliot Fine

LEFT *Scenic three-dimensional displays atop the entry to the Great Train Store attract railroad buffs of all ages.*

OPPOSITE
TOP *A model train moves along an overhead trestle.*
BOTTOM *Dark wood cabinetry and wood plank flooring are reminiscent of a vintage small-town railway station.*

ARENA ONE

BRISTOL, ENGLAND

Contractor
**Phoenix
Construction**

Photographer
Chris Hollick

A Leisure Department Store

FAMILY ENTERTAINMENT CENTERS REPRESENT A fast-growing market that is being targeted internationally. Arena One in Bristol, near the Bristol Channel on England's west coast, offers a broad selection of activities that can be enjoyed by the whole family. It is the first combined leisure and retail marketplace of its kind in the UK, and bills itself as a new-generation leisure department store for all ages.

The designers worked closely with the owners, First Leisure, to define a dynamic brand identity that reflects consumer trends and will build customer loyalty. Arena One incorporates a superbowl tenpin facility, a Sega Park amusement area, fast-food facilities, and Planet Kids, a separate children's play center.

To build a strong identity for Planet Kids, a set of comic characters was created. They appear on signage, at play points, and on all Planet Kids merchandise. The Planet Kids Store is adjacent to the main children's site within Arena One. Attractions include a 12-foot-high giant skittle icon, interactive learning, and soft play activities.

LEFT A combination of two- and three-dimensional exterior signs announce Arena One.

OPPOSITE
**TOP AND BOTTOM
LEFT** *An oversized bowling pin marks the entrance to the Superbowl.*
**RIGHT CENTER AND
BOTTOM** *The zooming rocket Planet Kids logo appears on T-shirts, shopping bags, and other items.*

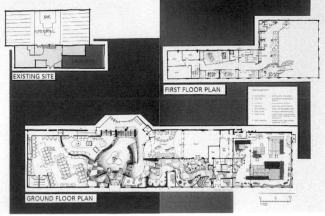

EXISTING SITE

FIRST FLOOR PLAN

GROUND FLOOR PLAN

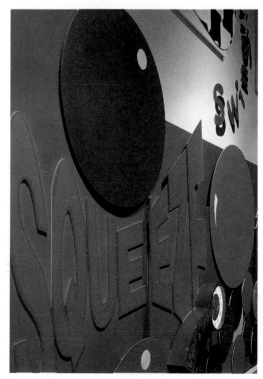

home

ANTHROPOLOGIE

ROCKVILLE, MARYLAND

Contractor

C.T. Management

*Special Finishes
and Materials*

Otto Installations

Photographer

©Tom Crane

LEFT *This vignette
features a vintage
metal panel over the
fireplace, mottled
walls, and spotlights
behind exposed wood
beams.*

OPPOSITE
TOP *Soft white
casement curtains con-
trast with a patterned
wall of randomly
placed bricks within
wood frames.*
BOTTOM *Display
fixtures incorporate
endposts made of
wood from old barns
and farmhouses.*

NEXT PAGE
*Anthropologie's presen-
tation combines the
look of a Mediterranean
seaside villa and a
country farmhouse.*

Masterfully Mediterranean

IF YOU LISTEN CLOSELY, YOU CAN ALMOST detect the sound of the Mediterranean
Sea lapping at the stony beach outside your villa. Or hear the horse-drawn cart
approaching your farmhouse in Provence. That's the effect achieved by the designers
of Anthropologie. They made the most of the store's 12,000 square feet and 22-foot-
high walls to create a bright and airy ambience so typical of the centuries-old
dwellings in southern France, Spain, and Italy.

PEARS

In addition to apparel and gifts, Anthropologie carries an eclectic selection of upscale products for home and garden. The merchandise appeals to sophisticated, well-travelled adults looking for good design from many cultures.

Natural materials and liberal use of texture form the background foil for vignettes, room settings, and product displays. For example, hand-mixed, pigment-rich plaster is textured with straw; wallpaper is treated to give a softly aged look; wainscoting, mosaic tiles, and a wall of timber is complemented with random brick infill; another wall of branches is woven through a timber grid. The floors are covered with weathered wood planks and terra-cotta tiles.

A series of vignettes along one wall is defined by foot-thick white frames that have the look of weathered stucco. Lively visual touches include a wall of antique country quilts framed by old barn wood, a fireplace with a rustic wood mantel, and exposed wood beams.

Photographer
George Mott

Lee Stout, Inc.

STEUBEN

WHITE SULPHUR SPRINGS, WEST VIRGINIA

A Crystalline Jewel

THE STEUBEN SHOP AT THE GREENBRIER RESORT was designed as the retail component of a marketing program to position the company as a leader in modern as well as traditional glass design. The materials selected for the interior architecture and the displays augment and amplify the brilliance of the crystal products.

The shop interior is framed by a neutral-color geometric band which begins at the storefront and continues inside to wrap the walls, floor and ceiling. Gold leaf wallcovering and a highly polished marble floor balance the modern aesthetic of light wood and elegant detailing. The result is a jewel-like setting for crystal treasures.

The most expensive and unusual pieces are shown on pedestals or in custom wall vitrines. Other Steuben pieces are displayed in open-front crystal shelves and on tabletops.

Lighting throughout the store is precisely controlled for focus, direction, and color temperature. Virtually every light in the shop is directed onto the merchandise, making each item appear like a star on its own stage-like platform. An internally illuminated cube of Steuben crystal cantilevered from a rear wall appears as a glowing beacon to draw shoppers' attention through the store and to the rear.

LEFT *The full-height glass storefront is accented by the precise geometry of the entry.*

OPPOSITE *An internally illuminated cube of Steuben crystal is cantilevered from a rear wall. Every light enhances the jewel-like qualities of the merchandise displayed in niches, vitrines, shelves, and on tables.*

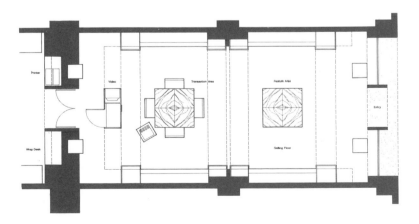

SIGNATURES HOMESTORE

CRESTVIEW HILL, KENTUCKY

Creative Settings

THE MERCHANDISING OF PRODUCTS FOR residential interiors often depends on effective nonverbal communication. Successful model rooms and vignettes not only reach out and draw shoppers into the showcased spaces, but involve their lifestyles and personal artistic expressions in the selection process.

Mercantile Stores launched Signatures, a sophisticated approach to home furnishings retailing, with a spacious, 36,000-square-foot store. The inventive, nontraditional space plan radiates from a central display island containing the featured model living room and vignettes from the Signatures collection. Customers are encouraged to

Contractor

Messer

Photographer

**Jamie Padgett/
Karant &
Associates, Inc.**

LEFT *The exterior
entrance to Signatures
Homestore utilizes
warm colors and
subtle textures.*

OPPOSITE
TOP *Regal colors and
dramatic accessories
accentuate the elegance
of this inspired bed-
room setting.*
BOTTOM *Freestanding
canted walls and
dropped ceiling
panels divide settings
and focus attention
on displays.*

explore the Century Gallery, Design Center, Carpets, Accessories, Lamps, Home Theater, Living Rooms, and Leather Gallery. Freestanding canted walls separate the rooms and displays. Overhead, dropped ceiling panels containing downlights focus attention on individual and grouped settings.

The broad, curved central staircase adds elegance to surrounding displays. Accessories, coordinated with room settings and vignettes, stimulate add-on sales. The overall design program included creating the Signatures name and logo, space planning, interior design, and visual merchandising.

BELOW *A sweeping staircase covered with a dark floral pattern carpet adds drama to adjacent displays.*

OPPOSITE *The graphic design for the spacious, 36,000-square-foot Signatures Homestore in the Crestview Hill Mall included its logo and the overall identity program.*

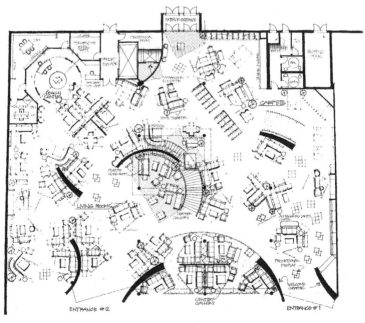

MAGASIN DU NORD

COPENHAGEN, DENMARK

Contractor

**Ednar Møller &
Sønner A/S**

Photographer

Torsten Høgh

Updated Danish Modern

COPENHAGEN'S MAGASIN DU NORD DEPARTMENT store is in the grand European manner—a block-long building in the French Second Empire style. Inside, "Form & Funktion," the new 4,700-square-foot (437-square-meter) housewares department is a mid-1990s interpretation of modern-classic Danish contemporary styling.

Unlike the current U.S. penchant for the "big box" look, Magasin Du Nord impresses shoppers with its broad selection, well-organized and uniformly present-ed—without a manufacturer's box in sight. The department carries kitchen utensils, informal dinnerware, glassware, small furniture items, and kitchen textiles.

The department shows merchandise on blond wood shelves, positioned on wall runners also made of blond wood. Low, double-tier display units on gray stone bases

LEFT *The Magasin Du Nord is Copenhagen's premier department store and a downtown architectural landmark.*

OPPOSITE

TOP *"Form & Funktion" signs, made of the same blond wood used extensively throughout the depart-ment, are suspended by burlap straps.*
BOTTOM *Merchandise displays are impressive for the breadth and depth of selection, and create an overall image of scrupulous tidiness.*

form mid-aisle displays. Flooring is mahogany; its rich brown tone is a pleasant contrast to the merchandise, which is primarily white or polished metal, with groupings in accent colors.

Form & Funktion's layout is based on a pathway plan which is well-suited to a single-level department of this size. A pathway plan is a good architectural organizer; shoppers are pulled smoothly from the front to the rear without interruption by floor fixtures. This type of plan thwarts a feeling of confusion that can disorient customers when confronted with a maze of merchandise.

Magasin du Nord's designers interpreted the pathway plan for Form & Funktion like a classic urban grid. Broad main "avenues" are intersected by wide "streets." With densely stocked shelves extending eight and nine levels up from their bases, the generously proportioned aisles maintain a comfortably open feeling in the department.

BELOW *Mahogany flooring is an effective contrast to the merchandise which is primarily white or polished metal with groupings in accent colors.*

OPPOSITE *Form & Funktion's broad main and secondary aisles maintain an open feeling in the densely stocked 4,700-square-foot department.*

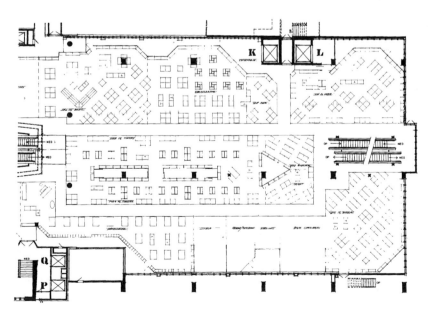

Photographer

Andrew Bordwin

Desgrippes Gobé & Associates

DREXEL HERITAGE HOME INSPIRATIONS

DREXEL, NORTH CAROLINA

Lifestyle Decor Center

MASS MARKET HOME FURNISHINGS STORES once concentrated on "suites" of furniture: five same-style pieces for the dining room; six for the bedroom; three for the living room. Eclectic taste was primarily for those who could afford interior design consultants to pull together furniture and accessories from diverse periods and influences to create a coordinated look. Now, consumers are better traveled, read shelter magazines, frequent auctions and antique shops, and prefer to exercise their own decorating tastes to suit their particular lifestyle.

Drexel Heritage is the retail arm of one of the country's leading home furnishings manufacturers. Its "Home Inspirations" prototype store not only encourages

LEFT *The exterior of the 20,000-square-foot, free-standing prototype store.*

OPPOSITE *A blond wood ramp leads customers up to the Design Center at the Drexel Heritage Home Inspirations store.*

134

world be a
good idea too.

And if there's
a style you'd
like, but just
don't see,

more chairs than

almost anyone.
And we'd

surely like to

LEFT *Curved dark
wood panels create
an elegant background
for the sample chair
display at the Drexel
Heritage Home
Inspirations store.*

OPPOSITE
TOP *Like pieces of
fine sculpture, sample
chairs can be examined
from all angles.*
BELOW *The graphic
image program
includes exterior
banners, stationery,
direct-mail pieces,
and shopping bags.*

purchasing, but also has an educational objective: to help customers find their lifestyle preferences in home decor by browsing, comparing, and evaluating.

The curved plan for the 20,000-square-foot, free-standing store has a raised Design Center as its core. Here, the customer has access to home decorating periodicals, resource books, computerized displays, and videos. Work tables and a coffee bar invite shoppers to consult with a Home Inspirations consultant, or to do their own home decor planning. A pair of curved, wood-frame walls displays hundreds of oversized fabric samples. Chair samples become part of a museum-like setting in front of a set of tall, dark wood panels. They define a colonnade pathway leading the customer past room settings and vignettes.

GARDEN RIDGE

AUSTIN, TEXAS

A Power Market for Home and Garden

WHEN TEXANS SET OUT TO DO SOMETHING NEW and different, they typically do it in a really big way. This 200,000-square-foot Garden Ridge megastore is the prototype for the eight-store chain operating in Texas, Oklahoma, and Kentucky (three units are the size of the Austin flagship store).

Occupying an entire former discount mall, the store covers the equivalent of three football fields. For crafts and home decorating customers, it is the destination shopping mecca for flowers, pottery, baskets, housewares, home accents, party supplies, and seasonal items.

One of the keys to the store's success is the organization of its departments and the sign system that helps shoppers negotiate their way around the selling floor without getting lost. Garden Ridge is like a city in microcosm, and its signage is commensurately arranged in layers, from large to small. Its first layer is composed of seven-and-a-half foot square, three-dimensional hanging signs showing an icon and

138

Lighting Consultant
Illuminating Concepts

Graphic Designer
Gail Nicklowitz

Signs and Banners
Neon Electric

Flooring
Flor-Tech

Photographer
Laszlo Regos

LEFT *Austin's 200,000-square-foot Garden Ridge, formerly a discount mall, is now a destination store for crafts and home decorating.*

OPPOSITE *Garden Ridge's flower department covers 30,000 square feet.*

the name of the department on a bright, solid color background that can be seen by customers throughout the store. The signs are color coded: the same background color is used for the smaller departmental signs, both hanging and headers. Uniform price information signs are black lettering on a yellow background.

The store's flooring is another design aspect that helps to guide shoppers. Concrete floors are painted in neutral colors within the departments and a vibrant red in the main aisles.

Twelve-foot high shelving is placed at the rear of the store and in some of the center areas. To prevent the canyon effect from tall shelving packed with merchandise, wider aisles and a higher light level give Garden Ridge shoppers more room to examine the massed displays. The design emphasizes the enormous selection to create a bright, festive, and fun shopping environment.

CENTRAL CARPET

NEW YORK CITY

Photography

**Courtesy of
Central Carpet**

A *"Grand Palais" of Rugs*

A CENTURY AFTER IT FIRST OPENED as the New York Bank for Savings, this landmark building in the city's Chelsea section has taken on a new life as Central Carpet's 40,000-square-foot retail store. Originally designed by architect R.H. Robertson in the Academic-Classic style popularized by the 1893 Chicago World's Columbian Exposition, its interior was restored to its former grandeur by an extensive adaptive reuse project.

The architects maintained the integrity of the original materials and design while providing a modern, efficient retail area equipped to display 15,000 rugs and carpets on customer-friendly racks. All display racks and fixtures are set away from the walls, a technique which leaves the original wall finishes intact. An additional selling level, which was added as a mezzanine that overlooks the original banking hall, is reached by a free-standing staircase. The staircase also leads down to the Rugskeller, the third selling level, displaying broadloom and the custom collection.

LEFT *Exotic rugs flank the view toward the Grand Mezzanine.*

OPPOSITE *Central Carpet's Main Hall has travertine-sheathed walls, Corinthian columns, a coffered ceiling, and a soaring, 60-foot-high dome.*

Photographer

Jaime Ardiles-Arce

DARIUS ANTIQUE RUGS

NEW YORK CITY

Star-quality Carpet Displays

FROM PRAYER RUGS TO ROOM-SIZE CARPETS, from antiques to contemporary, mounting distinctive visual displays of area rugs presents an on-going challenge to floor covering merchants. Darius Antique Rugs, a New York City trade resource and retail showroom, sponsors an annual event that attracts both designers and customers.

Leading interior designers and architects recently inducted into *Interior Design* magazine's Hall of Fame are invited to select a rug from the Darius collection and create a vignette incorporating furniture, lighting, and decorative accessories. Their settings—fanciful, dramatic, poetic, romantic, futuristic—demonstrate with flair and personal style that products with the same basic contour of length, width, and limited depth need not restrain imagination in their presentation.

LEFT *"Fret Not– Take Tea" Joseph Braswell, ASID. Mr. Braswell modeled his vignette on the Chinese tea house at Sans Souci in Potsdam, Germany. Chinese Chippendale-style wing chairs with fretwork backs flank a delicate antique Louis XV tray table. On the floor is a bold contemporary carpet with a stylized leopard pattern. A carved eighteenth-century chinoiserie terra-cotta sculpture on a pedestal placed in front of a mirror gives the illusion of extra depth. A crackle lacquer-finish screen contributes additional texture and dimension to the setting.*

TOP *"Inner Space"*
Carolyn Iu, Iu/Lewis
Designs, LLC.
For a space that could
be the corner of a
private library or a
small writing room,
Ms. Iu's display blend-
ed the patterns of a
Bakhshayesh carpet
on the floor and a
Chinese tapestry that
covers the feature wall.
Dark wood panels with
open fretwork add
visual impact to the
setting. The carved
eighteenth-century
Chinese desk is illumi-
nated by a polished
metal Deco-style table
lamp. The chair is the
Exeter by Knoll.

BOTTOM *"Learning to*
Live with Grace"
Kevin Walz, Walz
Design Inc.
Mr. Walz wove textures
with solids and voids to
create a room-size
sculpture. His presen-
tation mixes a twine
and velvet architectural
screen, tarpaper clap-
boarding, sandpaper
shingles, and sand-
blasted marine ply-
wood. An Agra carpet
covers the floor.

specialty retail

SOUTHWESTERN BELL

OH YES TORONTO

BORDERS BOOKS AND MUSIC

APPLE COMPANY STORE

COCA-COLA FIFTH AVENUE

SAM GOODY

BAY OF SPIRITS GALLERY

TEMPUS EXPEDITIONS

COMP*USA*

Contractor

Clyde Riggs

Photographer

**Bob Shimer,
Hedrich-Blessing**

Elliott + Associates Architects

SOUTHWESTERN· BELL

OKLAHOMA CITY, OKLAHOMA

PCS IS NOW

The Sky's the Limit

CELLULAR PHONE AND CELLULAR FACSIMILE MACHINES have made sophisticated wireless communication possible anywhere in the world. One of the first retail stores in the United States dedicated to wireless products occupies 2,300 square feet on the entry level of a 350,000-square-foot office building in downtown Oklahoma City. Elliott + Associates created a demonstration area and salesroom that dramatically highlights the virtually limitless opportunties for wireless communication. The

LEFT *A 32-foot-long interactive display table and rear "sky wall" dramatize the wireless communication products.*

OPPOSITE *Changes in lighting, color, and configuration invite customers into the street-level showroom and store.*

products are displayed as jewels of technology, positioned on wall-hung cabinets and on a 32-foot-long floating display table that functions as an interactive centerpiece. Emphasizing the "sky's the limit" theme is a two-sided "sky wall" that is visible in both the showroom and the conference room. North-facing, 16-foot-high windows are covered with perforated painted hardboard to focus the customer's attention on the interior environment and products.

PCS Is Now

PERSONAL COMMUNICATION SERVICES

ARE YOUR WINDOW ON A NEW WAY OF LIFE.

NOW YOU CAN REACH PEOPLE, NOT PLACES.

IT'S A WORLD OF CONVENIENCE AND EASE,

EFFICIENCY AND PEACE OF MIND.   YOU'RE

ALWAYS IN TOUCH,   ANYWHERE, ANYTIME.

Southwestern Bell Mobile Systems

PCS VALUE ZON

WE ALL TRAVEL IN WELL-WORN CIRCLE

IF YOUR CIRCLES CENTER MAIN

ON OKLAHOMA CITY'S DOWNTOWN A

SURROUNDING AREAS, YOU'RE IN T

PCS VALUE ZONE, AND YOU'RE A

CLEAR ADVANTAGE. WITH A LOW

RATE ON CALLS YOU MAKE IN TH

WIDELY TRAVELED AREA, YOUR CIRC

IS MORE AFFORDABLE THAN EVE

T ALL STARTS RIGHT HER

Contractor

**Salwood General
Contractors**

Photographer

**Design Archive/
Robert Burley**

OH YES TORONTO

TORONTO, CANADA

Above It All

ATTRACTING CUSTOMERS ON THE RUN calls for a bold visual merchandising approach. Oh Yes Toronto, a 400-square-foot store in busy Pearson International Airport, demonstrates a bold, tasteful format geared to spur impulse buying and facilitate rapid transaction turnover.

Large, multicolored letters in the store's logostyle are effectively positioned on a surface not usually utilized for graphics—the ceiling, which is sloped and cove-lit to increase visibility from the adjacent corridor.

Oh Yes Toronto's colorful and diverse product line is housed in a system of flexible components. Wall fixturing consists of a counter for display and folding, adjustable shelving and display panels, and fixed shelving for storage underneath. A coordinated material and color palette of white and natural maple visually maximizes the space.

152

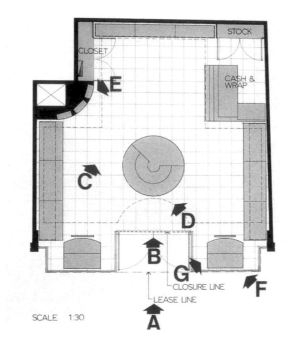

STOCK

CLOSET

CASH & WRAP

E

C

D

B

G

CLOSURE LINE

LEASE LINE

A

F

SCALE 1:30

BELOW *A white and maple scheme form a neutral backdrop for the colorful and varied stock.*

OPPOSITE

TOP *A curved display wall in maple veneer softens the store's squareness.* **BOTTOM LEFT, CENTER, AND RIGHT** *A flexible component system effectively houses Oh Yes Toronto's varied product line.*

Contractor

**Plant
Construction Co.**

Photographer

Vittoria Visuals

BORDERS BOOKS AND MUSIC

SAN FRANCISCO, CALIFORNIA

Words and Music on The Square

LOCATED ON SAN FRANCISCO'S UNION SQUARE, Borders Books & Music creates a lively environment with a distinctly urban flavor in a four-level, 34,000-square-foot store.

Borders, which shares the building's ground floor with other businesses, has a limited selling area for books and magazines on the street level. To draw shoppers to the upper levels, the designers installed a skylight above the escalators and colorful murals executed by airbrush in a WPA-style. They depict local landmarks and cultural icons,

LEFT *The new Borders logo adorns the exterior banners.*

OPPOSITE

TOP *Colorful murals depicting local landmarks and cultural icons are placed behind the cashwrap.*
BELOW LEFT AND RIGHT *Bookmarks, shopping bags, mugs, stickers, gift certificates, and other items exhibit the distinctive Borders logo.*

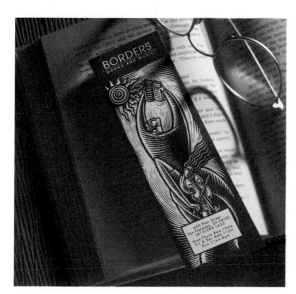

thereby reinforcing the store's connection to the local market. Additional murals in the same style appear behind the cashwrap and near the elevators.

Books and CDs are displayed in oak fixtures against creamy white walls and gold-colored carpeting. Reading nooks were placed throughout the store to provide intimate spaces for book selection. The extensive graphics and signage package created for Borders' Union Square store is now in use throughout the chain.

BELOW *Cafe Borders features an exposed brick wall, ceramic tile flooring, hanging pendant lamps, and oak furnishings. It overlooks Union Square.*

TOP AND BOTTOM

The in-store signage system is color coded to identify merchandise classifications.

159

Gensler

APPLE COMPANY STORE

CUPERTINO, CALIFORNIA

Photographer
Chas McGrath

Contractor
Rudolph + Sletten

Display Designer
Gensler

Graphic Designer
John Bricker

Lighting Designer
Auerback & Glasow

Ripe for Picking

THIS 3,500-SQUARE-FOOT COMPANY STORE is currently Apple Computer's sole venture into public retailing. Because of its location at the entrance to Apple's primary research and development campus, Gensler's designers took the opportunity to create not only a store, but a showcase for all of Apple's leading-edge products.

Visitors to the campus are introduced to the product array by a sweeping metallic curve of technology juxtaposed against a more traditional wood-veneer library wall display. Hardware and software from these displays are brought together on interactive kiosks positioned at the store's center.

At the back of the store, a series of neutral, mobile fixtures display souvenir items such as key rings, mugs, and T-shirts, at least one of which most visitors purchase before leaving the site. The shell of the space is finished in simple black and white, with accents of purple and red to set off the colorful Apple merchandise.

LEFT *Impulse items are grouped on mobile fixtures at the rear of the store.*

OPPOSITE
TOP *A curved wall of metallic gray painted columns dramatizes displays of Apple's product line.*
BOTTOM *An olive green perforated screen at the cashwrap is a solution to masking the plugs and wires on the computer's backside.*

Ronnette Riley Architect

COCA-COLA FIFTH AVENUE

NEW YORK CITY

Coke's Urban Image

COCA-COLA FIFTH AVENUE IN NEW YORK CITY establishes a special presence for the international soft drink producer on one of the world's premier shopping thorough-fares. The design of the store and the exhibit areas employ contemporary materials and lighting effects to highlight Coca-Cola's logo and merchandise.

The C-shaped, 150-foot-long space entices customers to experience its full length by following an illuminated "path" that combines a strong wall element, floor pattern, and ceiling treatment. An undulating ceiling ribbon alludes to the familiar white and

Lighting

Johnson Schwinghammer, Inc.

Display Consultants

Staples & Charles Ltd.

Graphic Designers

Margot Perman (with Ronnette Riley)

Logo Graphics

Landor Associates

Contractor

Sweet Construction

Photographer

Otto Baitz

LEFT *The story of Coca-Cola's history and global presence unfolds in the exhibits.*

OPPOSITE *Above the illuminated "path," a rolling white ceiling ribbon becomes red at night, and the edge-lit glass shelves glow Coke-bottle green.*

162

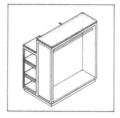
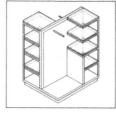
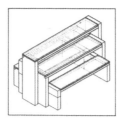

CUBES   CLOTHING FIXTURE I   CLOTHING FIXTURE II   NESTED TABLES

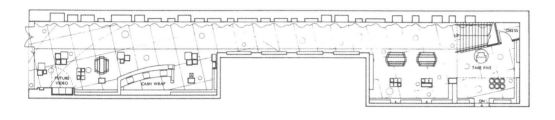

FURNITURE PLAN

0   5   10   20

silver underscore of the Coke logo; an electronically controlled dimming sequence sets the ribbon in motion, so that it appears to slowly roll toward the back stairway.

Coke's effervescence is also translated into the textured flooring of stainless steel. Exhibit area walls are leather and wood, providing a warm backdrop for showcases and antique reproductions. In the shop area, cool gray background hues make brightly colored merchandise stand out in vivid relief.

An interactive video displays flashbacks of world events interwoven with Coca-Cola history. The project received awards from the New York State Association of Architects/AIA and the Society of American Registered Architects.

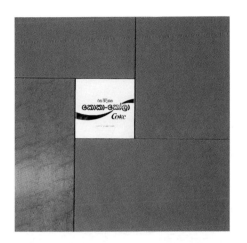

Musicland Group, Inc.

SAM GOODY

SAN DIEGO, CALIFORNIA

Goody Got It!

LESS THAN TWO MONTHS AFTER ITS LATE summer 1995 opening, the Sam Goody 32,000-square-foot supercombo store in San Diego's Horton Plaza became one of the top three stores in the 850-store chain. The soaring, dramatic space brings together visual rhythm, architectural overtones, innovative display accents, and spatial counterpoints that compose a symphony of sight, sound, and movement.

With angels and cherubs floating among the clouds above, and lighting providing warm luminosity, the spectacular environment gives the packaged CDs, videos, sound reproduction equipment and accessories a value-added presence that reaches out to customers.

After a Robinson's-May Department Store branch was vacated in 1993, Horton

Display Designer

The Jerde Partnership

Graphic Designer

Olio

Lighting Designer

Kaplan Architectural Lighting

Contractor

Johnson & Jennings

Architect

RSP Architects

Photographer

Brewster & Brewster Photography

LEFT *Five major zones were created: Popular Music, Classical Music, Movies, Books, and the Café.*

OPPOSITE *Sam Goody in Horton Plaza is located in a former department store branch that was subdivided for several major retail tenants.*

166

Plaza's owners, The Hahn Company, subdivided the structure and added a fourth level. Sam Goody, Planet Hollywood, Warner Brothers, and The Limited became tenants. Sam Goody occupies large portions of the first two levels with access from the third level. The existing escalator system was incorporated into the store's new design scheme. Renovation and redesign, completed at a per-square-foot cost of $93.75, or $3 million, created a fun, entertaining environment, with easy circulation and visual excitement.

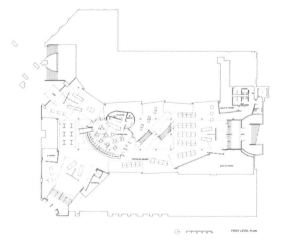

Contractor

**Elton General
Contracting, Inc.**

Photographer

David Whittaker

II By IV Design Associates Inc.

BAY OF SPIRITS GALLERY

TORONTO, CANADA

A Showcase for Native Canadian Art

AVOIDING THE STEREOTYPICAL RUSTIC CLICHÉS often associated with native art settings, the 1,400-square-foot Bay of Spirits Gallery is devoted to the display of Canadian art from the West Coast and other regions. The designers stretched their tight, $60-per-square-foot budget to create a comfortable environment that makes the artwork more accessible for both experienced and new collectors.

Space is provided for many different functions, such as exhibiting pieces on the walls and on various horizontal surfaces; an information and cashwrap with computer; special collections area; wearable art area; storage and shipping room; private office; and merchandising units for jewelry, pottery, and small sculpture. Totems, paintings, masks, and small items are all sensitively displayed using minimal floor space.

LEFT *The traditional ovoid form of the Canadian Northwest is repeated in the cash-wrap, which is faced with birch bark.*

OPPOSITE
TOP LEFT *A mosaic of the gallery's logo is set into earth-colored carpet at the entrance, leading customers into the main display areas.*
TOP RIGHT *Spotlights add impact to a mounted display of masks.*
BOTTOM LEFT *A curved birch platform is backed by three partial walls of heavy natural lumber.*
BOTTOM RIGHT *Small objects are displayed in glass cases atop natural cedar log pedestals.*

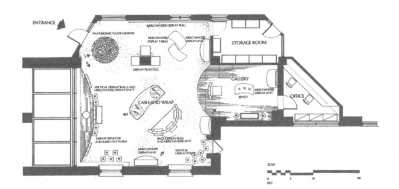

TEMPUS EXPEDITIONS

BLOOMINGTON, MINNESOTA

Developer
**Fortney &
Weygandt**

Simulation
Equipment
Moog, Inc.

Photographer
Dan Forer

A Supercharged Selling Environment

TEMPUS EXPEDITIONS INTRODUCES A COMBINATION of entertainment, education, and retailing to a dramatically-themed mall environment. For the 5,000-square-foot prototype store and theater in the Mall of America, the designers integrated high-definition digital technology, retail presentation of discovery-inspired merchandise, three-dimensional virtual audio, electronic motion simulation, and dramatic special effects.

Underlying the merchandise selection are the dual themes of exploration and achievement. The drive for human achievement is exemplified by a sprinting, larger-than-life, three-dimensional figure who has one leg in the mall corridor and the other

LEFT *The entrance to the 5,000-square-foot prototype store in the Mall of America.*

OPPOSITE *A male sprinter appears to vault through one of the show windows of Tempus Expeditions at the Mall of America. The quotation on the front window is from Shakespeare's As You Like It.*

172

leg inside the store as he appears to run through the glass show window.

A freestanding statue of Venus (given new mechanical arms) is poised at the center of a circular merchandise display. A domed moon hole cut into the ceiling and a circular pattern in the carpet adds to the ethereal setting.

To symbolize human invention, the designers hung giant reproductions of mechanical gears from the ceiling and then repeated the patterns on the terrazzo flooring.

LEFT *Beneath illustrations of famous explorers, visitors have the opportunity to interface with Scroll-O-Matic terminals.*

OPPOSITE

TOP LEFT *Strong colors and bright illumination add to the store's high energy level.*
TOP RIGHT *Freestanding display modules are topped with the store's logo.*
BOTTOM LEFT *Stylized Ionic capitals support shelf displays. The floor pattern is created by white letters and numerals on a purple background.*
BOTTOM RIGHT *The visual identity package includes logo, stationery, signage, packaging and labeling.*

Contractor

Ameribuild Construction Management Inc.

Photographer

Peter Paige

COMP*USA*

NEW YORK CITY

Electronics Retailing on Fifth Avenue

THIS TWO-LEVEL, 26,000-SQUARE-FOOT CompUSA UNIT brings the concept of suburban "big-box" warehouse merchandising to one of the world's most celebrated shopping streets, New York City's Fifth Avenue. The design had to address both the store's warehouse pricing and product nature, and the Class A corporate office building in which it is located. CompUSA occupies two-thirds of the ground level retail space, spanning 159 linear feet.

An enclosed billboard for merchandising and display was created by the corner wall, clearly seen by foot and vehicular traffic. Inside, the stairway and curved wall invite customers upstairs to view additional merchandise.

Most floor display units have a crisp, black metal finish; red is the accent color used

LEFT *The exterior of the two-level, 26,000-square-foot CompUSA at 38th Street and Fifth Avenue is a virtual retail billboard.*

OPPOSITE *Basic black metal display units are accented by red, four-way, free-standing fixtures. Back-lit fascia signs are red and white.*

for four-way, freestanding fixtures. At shoulder height, the display racks allow for maximum through-store visibility. The interior store signage on the fascia of the wall shelf units is back-lit white lettering on a red background. CompUSA installed video monitors that carry sales messages to the street in a changing display.

directory

STORES

Alain Mikli/Optique
878-880 Madison Avenue
New York, New York 10022
United States
Tel: (212) 472-6085

Ann Taylor Loft
723 Tanger Drive, #512
Riverhead, New York 11901
United States
Tel: (516) 369-8800

Anthropologie
11500 Rockville Pike
Rockville, Maryland 20852
United States
Tel: (301) 230-6520

Apple Company Store
1 Infinite Loop
Cupertino, California 95014
United States
Tel: (408) 996-1010

Arena One
Ashton Gate
Bristol
England
Tel: 011-79-538538

Bay of Spirits Gallery
156 Front Street West
Toronto, Ontario M5J ZL6
Canada
Tel: (416) 971-5190

Bloomingdale's
Mall of America
3000 Southeast Court
Bloomington, Minnesota 55435
United States
Tel: (612) 883-2600

Bloor Street Hosiery
50 Bloor Street West
Toronto, Ontario M4W 3L8
Canada
Tel: (416) 972-0697

Borders Books & Music
400 Post Street
San Francisco, California 94102
United States
Tel: (313) 995-7262

Boyd's
1818 Chestnut Street
Philadelphia, Pennsylvania 19103
United States
Tel: (215) 564-9000

Britches Great Outdoors
34 Market Square
Annapolis, Maryland 21401
United States
Tel: (410) 268-0177

Carlos Falchi
402 North Park Center
Dallas, Texas 75225
United States
Tel: (214) 368-7794

Central Carpet
81 Eighth Avenue
New York, New York 10011
United States
Tel: (212) 741-3700

Coca-Cola Fifth Avenue
711 Fifth Avenue
New York, New York 10022
United States
Tel: (212) 418-9692

CompUSA
420 Fifth Avenue
New York, New York 10018
United States
Tel: (212) 764-6224

Danskin Factory Store
Woodbury Commons Factory Outlet
Route 32, Store A-31
Central Valley, New York 10917
United States
Tel: (914) 928-4490

Darius Antique Rugs
38 East 57th Street
New York, New York 10022
United States
Tel: (212) 644-6600

Dayton Hudson
Burnsville Shopping Center
14251 Burnhaven Road
Burnsville, Minnesota 55337
United States
Tel: (612) 435-4801

**Drexel Heritage
Home Inspirations**
101 North Main Street
Drexel, North Carolina 28619
United States
Tel: (704) 433-3127

Fila Flagship Store
331 Powell Street
San Francisco, California 94102
United States
Tel: (415) 956-3452

Garden Ridge
2800 South IH 35
Round Rock, Texas 78681
United States
Tel: (512) 310-1130

Giorgio Beverly Hills
327 North Rodeo Drive
Beverly Hills, California 90210
United States
Tel: (310) 315-3191

Great Pacific Patagonia
1048 Wisconsin Avenue, N.W.
Washington, D.C. 20007
United States
Tel: (202) 333-1776

The Great Train Store
Crossgates Mall
#1 Crossgates Mall Road, #B-129
Albany, New York 12203
United States
Tel: (518) 869-1524

Hush Puppies Direct
Horizon Outlet Center
1695 94th Drive
Vero Beach, Florida 32966-3083
United States
Tel: (561) 569-6424

Jess Stores
5 rue Dosne
75016 Paris
France
Tel: 33-147-04-4441

**The Lake Forest Shop
Boutique**
265 East Market Square
Lake Forest, Illinois 60045
United States
Tel: (847) 234-0548

La Maison Simons
Les Galeries de la Capitale
5401 Boulevard de Galeries
Quebec City, Quebec
Canada
Tel: (418) 692-3630

London Fog Kids
Outlets at Gilroy
681 Leavesky Road
Gilroy, California 95020
United States
Tel: (408) 842-8215

Ludwig Beck AG
Marien Platz 8
D- 80264 Munich
Germany
Tel: 011-49-89-236910

Magasin du Nord
Kgs. Nytorv 13
1095 Copenhagen
Denmark
Tel: 4533114433

Mark Cross Outlet Store
739 Reading Road
West Reading, Pennsylvania 19611
United States
Tel: (610) 376-8634

Nex.is
6 Scotts Road Level 3 & 4
Scotts Shopping Centre
Singapore 0922
Tel: 7350030

Oh Yes Toronto
Pearson International Airport
Terminal 3
Toronto, Ontario
Canada
Tel: (416) 672-8554

**Oilily
Somerset Collection**
2801 West Big Beaver Road C157
Troy, Michigan 48084
United States
Tel: (810) 614-9030

The Quality Shop
Hilltop East Shopping Center
1556 Laskin Road, Suite 138
Virginia Beach, Virginia 23451
United States
Tel: (804) 428-8615

Sam Goody
199 Horton Plaza
San Diego, California 92100
United States
Tel: (619) 233-0890

Signatures Homestore
Crestview Hill Mall
2901 Dixie Highway
Crestview Hill, Kentucky 41017
United States
Tel: (606) 344-2853

Southwestern Bell
20 North Broadway
Oklahoma City, Oklahoma 73102
United States
Tel: (405) 858-2590

Steuben
The Greenbrier Hotel
300 West Main Street
White Sulphur Springs,
West Virginia 24986
United States
Tel: (304) 536-1110

Tangs Studio
391-B Orchard Road
Nee Ann City 238874
Singapore
Tel: (65) 235-7404

Tempus Expeditions
Mall of America
60 East Broadway
Bloomington, Minnesota 55425
United States
Tel: (612) 883-8936

The Tortoise and the Hare
1470 York Avenue
New York, New York 10021
United States
Tel: (212) 472-3399

Twinkles
Tysons Corner Shopping Center
2 Chain Bridge Road
McLean, Virginia
United States

Urban Outfitters
935 North Rush Steet
Chicago, Illinois 60611
United States
Tel: (312) 640-1919

ARCHITECTS & DESIGNERS

Michael Alain
LeMay & Michaud
111 rue St. Pierre
Quebec City, Quebec
Canada
Tel: (418) 694-1010
Fax: (418) 694-1100

**Bentz, Thompson,
Rietow, Inc.**
2600 Foshay Tower
Minneapolis, Minnesota 55402
United States
Tel: (612) 332-1234
Fax: (612) 332-1813

Joseph Braswell
425 East 57th Street
New York, New York 10022
United States
Tel: (212) 698-1075

Brennan Beer Gorman Monk/Interiors
515 Madison Avenue
New York, New York 10022
United States
Tel: (212) 888-7667
Fax: (212) 935-3868

Charles E. Broudy and Associates
224 South 20th Street
Philadelphia, Pennsylvania 19103
United States
Tel: (215) 563-8488
Fax: (215) 568-6719

Desgrippes Gobé & Associates
411 Lafayette Street
New York, New York 10003
United States
Tel: (212) 979-8900
Fax: (212) 979-1401

Design Forum
3484 Far Hills Avenue
Dayton, Ohio 45429
United States
Tel: (513) 298-4400
Fax: (513) 294-2842

Diedrich Architects and Associates
3399 Peachtree Road, Suite 820
Atlanta, Georgia 30326
United States
Tel: (404) 364-9633
Fax: (404) 364-0064

Elliott + Associates Architects
35 Harrison Avenue
Oklahoma City, Oklahoma 73104
United States
Tel: (405) 232-9554
Fax: (405) 232-9997

Carlos Falchi
LGF Design Studio
44 West 18th Street
New York, New York 10011
United States
Tel: (212) 366-4666
Fax: (212) 366-9801

Fisher Gordon Architects
1032 Wisconsin Avenue, N.W.
Washington, D.C. 20007
United States
Tel: (202) 333-9270
Fax: (202) 337-7540

Fitch
Commonwealth House
1 New Oxford Street
London WC1A 1WW
England
Tel: (0171) 208-8027
Fax: (0171) 208-0200

Fitch Inc.
10350 Olentangy River Road
Worthington, Ohio 43085
United States
Tel: (614) 885-3453
Fax: (614) 885-4289

Fitzpatrick Design Group, Inc.
2109 Broadway, Suite 203
New York, New York 10023
United States
Tel: (212) 580-5842
Fax: (212) 580-5849

Fleeger Inc.
131 East 23rd Street
New York, New York 10010
United States
Tel: (212) 477-5729
Fax: (212) 228-2136

FRCH Design Worldwide
860 Broadway
New York, New York 10003
United States
Tel: (212) 254-1229
Fax: (212) 982-5543

FRCH Design Worldwide
311 Elm Street
Cincinnati, Ohio 45202
United States
Tel: (513) 241-3000
Fax: (513) 241-5051

Freebairn-Smith & Associates
442 Post Street
San Francisco, California 94102
United States
Tel: (415) 398-4094

Gensler
600 California Street
San Francisco, California 94108
United States
Tel: (415) 627-3737

The Great Train Store Company
14180 Dallas Parkway, Suite 618
Dallas, Texas 75240
United States
Tel: (214) 392-1599
Fax: (214) 392-1698

Marc-Henri Hecht
6 Av. de Lowendal
75007 Paris
France
Tel: 33.1 45 5590 15

Imaginari
1437 7th Street, Suite 340
Santa Monica, California 90401
United States
Tel: (310) 393-9111
Fax: (310) 458-2843

The International Design Group
188 Avenue Road
Toronto, Ontario M5R 2J1
Canada
Tel: (416) 961-1811
Fax: (416) 961-9734

Carolyn Iu
Iu and Lewis Designs, LLC
57 East 11th Street
New York, New York 10003
United States
Tel: (212) 982-3633

Jon Greenberg & Associates Inc.
29355 Northwestern Highway
Southfield, Michigan 48034
United States
Tel: (810) 355-0890
Fax: (810) 355-0895

Kiku Obata & Company
5585 Pershing Avenue, Suite 240
St. Louis, Missouri 63112
United States
Tel: (314) 361-3110
Fax: (314) 361-4716

Lee Stout, Inc.
348 West 36th Street
New York, New York 10018
United States
Tel: (212) 594-4563
Fax: (212) 268-5579

Magasin du Nord Store Planning
Kgs. Nytorv 13
1095 Copenhagen
Denmark
Tel: 4533114433

Mathias Thörner Design
40 West 22nd Street
New York, New York 10010
United States
Tel: (212) 675-1170
Fax: (212) 675-9061

Musicland Group, Inc.
10400 Yellow Circle Drive
Minnetonka, Minnesota 55343
United States
Tel: (612) 931-8026
Fax: (612) 931-8038

Pompei A.D.
394 West Broadway, 2nd Floor
New York, New York 10012
United States
Tel: (212) 431-1262
Fax: (212) 966-8659

Robert Scarano Associates
216 Hall Street
Brooklyn, New York 11205
United States
Tel: (718) 398-4338
Fax: (718) 398-4406

Ronnette Riley Architect
350 Fifth Avenue, #8306
New York, New York 10118
United States
Tel: (212) 594-4015
Fax: (212) 594-2868

RSP Architects
120 First Avenue North
Minneapolis, Minnesota 55401
United States
Tel: (612) 339-0313
Fax: (612) 339-6760

Timothy Higgins Design
94 George Street
Harrington Park, New Jersey 07640
United States
Tel: (201) 784-2153
Fax: (201) 784-2153

Tobin/Parnes Design Enterprises
270 Lafayette Street, Suite 302
New York, New York 10012
United States
Tel: (212) 941-9800
Fax: (212) 941-9810

Trauth Associates Ltd.
1550 N. Northwest Highway, Suite 333
Park Ridge, Illinois 60068
United States
Tel: (847) 827-9300
Fax: (847) 827-9329

II by IV Design Associates Inc.
77 Mowat Avenue, Suite 109
Toronto, Ontario M6K3E3
Canada
Tel: (416) 531-224
Fax: (416) 531-4460

Kevin Walz
Walz Design Inc.
20 West 20th Street
New York, New York 10011
United States
Tel: (212) 229-2299

PHOTOGRAPHERS

Jaime Ardiles-Arce
730 Fifth Avenue, 9th floor
New York, New York 10019
United States
Tel: (212) 333-8779
Fax: (212) 593-2070

Paul Bielenberg
Bielenberg & Associates
6823 Pacific View Drive
Los Angeles, California 90068
United States
Tel: (213) 874-9951
Fax: (213) 874-1907

Andrew Bordwin
70A Greenwich Street
New York, New York 10011
United States
Tel: (212) 285-2158
Fax: (212) 633-1046

Brewster & Brewster Photography
429½ California Avenue
Glendale, California 91203
United States
Tel: (818) 956-3717
Fax: (818) 956-0530

Robert Burley
Design Archive
276 Carlaw Avenue, #219
Toronto, Ontario
Canada
Tel: (416) 466-0211
Fax: (416) 465-2592

Peter Chen
Chen Shan Company
Telok Blangah East
P.O. Box 209
Singapore 9109
Tel: 274-3733
Fax: 271-1985

Tom Crane
113 Cumberland Place
Bryn Mawr, Pennsylvania 19010
United States
Tel: (610) 525-2444
Fax: (610) 527-7529

Don DuBroff
Fitzpatrick Design Group, Inc.
2109 Broadway, Suite 203
New York, New York 10023
United States
Tel: (312) 935-9007

Hans Georg Esch
Neiderichstrasse 34
D-50668 Cologne
Germany
Tel: (49) 221-121116
Fax: (49) 221-134760

Elliot Fine
100 Hudson Street
New York, New York 10013
United States
Tel: (212) 966-8614

Dan Forer
1970 NE 149th Street
North Miami, Florida 33181
United States
Tel: (305) 949-3131
Fax: (305) 949-3701

Stephen Graham
1120 West Stadium Boulevard #2
Ann Arbor, Michigan 48103
United States
Tel: (313) 761-6888

Timothy Higgins
94 George Street
Harrington Park, New Jersey 07640
United States
Tel: (201) 784-2153
Fax: (201) 784-2153

Torsten Høgh
Bygade 9E
3220 Tisulleeude
Denmark
Tel: 42309035

Chris Hollick
40 Montague Road
Southall Middlesex UB2 5PD
England
Tel: 44 181 843 9493

Steve Foxall
6132 Belmont Avenue
Dallas, Texas 75214
United States
Tel: (214) 824-1977
Fax: (214) 930-9121

Alan Karchmer
3400 Patterson Street, N.W.
Washington, D.C. 20015
United States
Tel: (202) 244-7511

Balthazar Korab
Korab Hedrich-Blessing
 Photographers
P.O. Box 895
5051 Beach Road
Troy, Michigan 48099
United States
Tel: (810) 952-1970
Fax: (810) 641-8889

Chun Y Lai
428 Broome Street
New York, New York 10013
United States
Tel: (212) 966-5025
Fax: (212) 966-5090

Glen McClure
2113 Colonial Avenue
Norfolk, Virginia 23517
United States
Tel: (804) 623-4046
Fax: (804) 623-3406

Chas McGrath
347 Corland Court
Santa Rosa, California 95404
United States
Tel: (707) 664-9980
Fax: (707) 664-9981

Micheal P. McLaughlin
P.O. Box 1622
Canal Street Station
New York, New York 10013
United States
Tel: (212) 334-0411

George Mott
122 West 26th Street
New York, New York 10001
United States
Tel: (212) 242-2753

Jamie Padgett
Karant & Associates, Inc.
400 North May Street
Chicago, Illinois 60622
United States
Tel: (312) 733-0891
Fax: (312) 733-1781

Peter Paige
269 Parkside Road
Harrington Park, New Jersey 07640
United States
Tel: (201) 767-3150
Fax: (201) 767-9263

Palladium Photo Design
Stephanstrasse 7-9
D-50676 Cologne
Germany
Tel: (49) 221-247608
Fax: (49) 221-218251

David Patterson
Box 85
81 Mesa Street
Jamestown, Ohio 80455
United States
Tel: (303) 442-9029

Laszlo Regos
3127 West Twelve Mile Road
Berkley, Michigan 48072
United States
Tel: (810) 398-3631
Fax: (810) 398-3997

Michael Roberts
1314 West Randolph Street
Chicago, Illinois 60607
United States
Tel: (312) 829-7499
Fax: (312) 829-9865

Bob Shimer
Hedrich-Blessing
11 West Illinois
Chicago, Illinois 60610
United States
Tel: (312) 321-1151
Fax: (312) 321-1165

Mark Steele
Fitch Inc.
10350 Olentangy River Road
Worthington, Ohio 43085
United States
Tel: (614) 885-3453
Fax: (614) 885-4289

Studio Clark
24 rue Pasteur
Ivry/Seine
France
Tel: 45 21 01 18

Vittoria Visuals
2400 Pacific Avenue, #802
San Francisco, California 94115
United States
Tel: (415) 921-1102
Fax: (415) 921-1114

Matt Wargo
Charles E. Broudy and Associates
224 South 20th Street
Philadelphia, Pennsylvania 19103
United States
Tel: (215) 563-8488
Fax: (215) 568-6719

David Whittaker
11 Carlaw Avenue, Unit Three
Toronto, Ontario M4M2R6
Canada
Tel: (416) 466-0558
Fax: (416) 466-0989

index

acknowledgments

Our fondest thanks to the *Retail Store Image* staff—John Davis, Robin Marchetti, Amie Leibovitz, Michelle Koerner, Kari Hudson, Paige Johnson, Liz Jensen Daws, and Terri Hill—for sharing our commitment to image.

Vilma Barr
Katherine Field

STORES